THE
POWER
OF 1

Living the life that Counts

BANKOLE AKINLADE

Copyright © Enability Press 2013
Bankole Akinlade has asserted his right under the Copyright, Designs and Patents Act 1988 to be identified as the author of this work.

ISBN: 978-0-9575885-1-6
Published by Enability Press
info@enability.org
Printed in the United Kingdom

REVIEWS

I feel extremely honoured by God to be holding this book in my hand. Bankole is indeed a true son of the Ministry, and his message amplifies themes that I have taught and been passionate about for many years.

I believe that this is Bankole's best book yet. Enjoy the read and be provoked to lead a life that counts .

Dr Sola Fola-Alade.
Senior Pastor, Trinity Chapel. London

Whatever your life experiences, good or bad, and regardless of how limited your opportunities might be, you are able to accomplish something significant. Bankole offers a blueprint for living a life that matters, to help you do just that.

Errol Lawson
Author of 'From The Postcode to the Globe - How to overcome limitations and realise your potential'

This book is dedicated to:

Abel Kolapo Akinlade – My biological father.
Your words, 'remember whose son you are',
still ring true today and their meaning is even clearer.
I have not forgotten.

Thank you.

Dr Sola Fola-Alade – My spiritual father.
Benjamin Disraeli said, "the greatest good you can do for
another is not just to share your riches but to reveal to him
his own." Thank you for revealing my riches to me.

FOREWORD

Congratulations Bankole, on the release of this wonderful book! Thank you for writing this book, at a time that many have moved away from the truth to error, thinking all that glitters is gold and believing that what you acquire materially equates to success.

My introduction to Bankole was through his first book "Leading the Right Side Up: How to lead when you are not the boss" given to me by his Pastor. On reading the book, I was not disappointed. He is a man of purpose with a simple but challenging and progressive message.

When he speaks, one cannot help but listen. He is a faithful armour-bearer to his Pastor.

He is one of the treasured gifts in the body of Christ that caught the revelation of what real success is.

Through this book, he has redefined success God's way. He presents the notion that you are not successful because of what you have, but by the lives you impact. Success is also the mark you leave in people's lives while living or after you are dead.

Simply put, 'who will miss you and why will you be missed?'

As a follower of Jesus Christ, it is established that being called a christian is not enough. Quoting the scripture means nothing if your life is not lived according to what scripture says. After all, the scripture teaches us that faith without works is dead.

The Power of One presents us with the details of the lives of men who changed others' lives or made a positive difference to their world. These were individuals like you and I, who were not content with just breathing and making money but wanted to leave a legacy.

Thank you for not sitting on the fence or being comfortable in your church, Bankole. Instead you dared to take the bull by the horns in order to tackle sensitive issues that are costing generations an untold waste of human and material resources.

We are not on earth by accident. We are relevant to our world and I believe through this book, there will be an awakening in our spirits and souls to leave a mark, both while we are alive and after we are dead!

Lola Oyebade
Senior Pastor, House On The Rock
International Church London.

PREFACE

I had just emerged from a prolonged 'valley experience' and now, life looked good- everything was looking up. I was dating the woman of my dreams, and my future looked certain. Everything I thought I had lost was coming together. To be honest, I could not have wished for anything more, it seemed as if all my prayers were being answered at once. One nice summer afternoon, I excitedly asked my then-fiancée to accompany me to view the newly built apartment that I intended to buy. I wanted it to be our first home, so I was eager to get her views on it. She loved it. We surveyed the interior of the apartment and discussed the finishing touches we would like to add. Our conversation soon turned to our future together and I started sharing some of my dreams and hopes. I'd talked about my hopes for the future many times before, but there was something different about this time. I barely got going before I started to sob like a little child. My reaction took me by surprise and I was so embarrassed by my childlike behaviour. Here I was, on the cusp of a major milestone in my life, and yet, I felt so down. It took me a while to understand what was happening to me. I realised that while all these material blessings from God were great, something was missing. I longed for fulfilment, for a life of significance, but none of these things seemed to hold the key to such a life. It was as if God was showing me that I could have all the material blessings He promised but remain unfulfilled. This was a profound revelation.

I realised that what I really wanted was not so much the trappings of success, but to live a life full of meaning. I wanted my life to make a difference and to count for something beyond me. Subsequently, Jesus began to teach me, using the parable in the bible of the 'rich fool', that a man's life does not consist in the abundance of his possessions [1]. This idea was so antithetical to what I had grown up believing. I knew no other way to measure a man's success than to look at the qualifications he had acquired, positions he held and the wealth he had accumulated. Perhaps this outlook was unsurprising given the way popular culture portrays success.

Jesus told the parable of the 'rich fool' after he had been asked to mediate a feud related to the sharing of a family inheritance. I don't think Jesus was opposed to the idea of inheritance or its equitable sharing, I think what He was trying to do, in His characteristic way, was to deal with the underlying motives of those involved. So, he told the story of the rich fool, who was preoccupied with accumulating wealth with no thought for how it might improve the lives of others. Jesus was teaching that in life, it is not what one acquires and keeps that matters. In the story, an important question is posed to the rich fool and I think it's a pertinent one for each of us to consider:

But God said to him, 'Fool! This night your soul will be required of you; then whose will those things be which you have provided? "So *is* he who lays up treasure for himself, and is not rich toward God.- Luke 12: 20 - 21

The rich fool was making long-term plans, expecting that he would live long enough to enjoy his wealth, but Jesus pointed out that the length of his life was out of his hands. Jesus was not against the idea of planning, but He wanted to draw attention to what really matters - planning for an eternal legacy.

Making plans for an eternal legacy is not something we talk about enough; it is often left in the domain of religion. Proponents of secularism and humanism would have us believe that, here on earth is where it all ends and that the decisions we make do not have any eternal significance. On the other hand, the church often teaches us to be heaven-focused, so much so that our relevance on earth is often greatly diminished. The goal of this book is to highlight the importance of what we do on earth in shaping our eternal legacy because the truth is it's not a choice *between* heaven and earth, our focus must encompass *both*.

The scope of this book has evolved over the years and, I believe, has matured into something of greater significance than I initially envisioned. This maturing process has mirrored the transformation of my own thoughts on the subject. Through various experiences with God, I've discovered a clearer narrative for my life as I sojourn on this side of eternity.I have shared many of these experiences in this book.

When I began writing this book, I came across a number of books with similar titles, but their approach to the subject is very different to the one I have taken. I hope the thoughts I share here will cause you to begin to see yourself differently. I also hope it will trigger, or at least contribute to, a whole new perspective on the purpose of life and help you discover ways to make a difference that counts for eternity.

ACKNOWLEDGEMENT

T hough I have titled this book The Power of One, I have learnt that a good book is never a solo effort. It requires the power of a team.

The idea to write this book was first conceived about six years ago. It might have died before I even started writing it, but for the encouragement of my friend, Dr Christianna Dinah. Thank you.

I consider myself most privileged to have a soulmate and helpmate, such as I have in my wife. Her presence in my life reassures me of my special place in God's heart. Her assistance in preparing the manuscript for publishing and, just as importantly, in cheering me on, made it possible for me to complete this work. Indeed, she was both my editor in-chief, and my Chief Encouragement Officer (CEO).

Neither my first book, Leading the Right Side Up, nor this one would have been published quite as I'd envisioned them, without the assistance of my editor, Ade Adewunmi. She has a knack for grasping the essence of the ideas I am seeking to convey and suggesting better ways to articulate them. Her work on the first book made it more easily comprehensible, and given the work we have put into The Power of One, I am confident of a similar outcome. I am most grateful for her valuable critique, and the relentless effort she put into the editing of this book to ensure that its readers are enriched.

Rebecca Ayanfalu and Olugbenga Pedro joined the team for last leg of the editorial work, but their contributions were no less significant. I am grateful for the time they took to read the manuscript and for their insightful comments and suggestions.

Lastly, I acknowledge God's grace upon my life and the inspiration given to me for the writing of this book and I offer it up in thanks. All the credit for any value derived from this book belongs to Him.

CONTENTS

INTRODUCTION

The life we are given is short;
but the memory of a well-spent life is eternal.
- Anonymous

The atmosphere was sombre; deep loss was etched on the faces of those gathered in the room. The occasion was a Service of Songs, held in honour of a gentleman who passed away soon after his fortieth birthday. His untimely death was a big shock to those who knew him. Shortly before his demise he had been told by his doctor that he was in robust health. He was on the verge of a major advancement in his career. His future looked promising, but unfortunately, his plans never came to pass.

Seated in the hall were the wife and daughter he left behind, as well as close family members and friends. While it was obvious they were mourning a great loss, many seemed to take solace in the knowledge that although he was gone, he would live on in their hearts. That day, as I sat listening to the eulogy, I found myself contemplating the deeper meaning of life. I suppose there's something about ceremonies such as these that trigger this sort of soul searching.

The ancient king, Solomon said, "it is better to go to a house of mourning than to go to a house of feasting, for death is the destiny of everyone; the living should take this to heart"[1]. This verse resonates with me because occasions such as the service described above leave me with a sobering determination to love more, live more and to leave an enduring legacy.

Several years ago, I came across a quote by Horace Mann, an American education reformer: "Be ashamed to die before you have won some victory for humanity". These words affected me greatly and I was so inspired by them that I decided to put them up on my bedroom wall. While I had no plans to die anytime soon, his words continually challenged me to make a positive difference in the lives of others.

The man whose life was being commemorated at the service I described above, only lived for forty short years yet it appeared that he managed to make a significant impact on the lives of others. I never met him, but it was evident from what was said about him during the service that he had left an indelible mark on those who knew him. One of the ladies who eulogized him recalled that he would always say to her, 'be the best you can be'. Another gentleman described him as someone who was, "... always there on the other end of the phone when you needed someone to talk to, regardless of where he was in the world at the time".

The people that make the most of their lives are those who realise that their life must count for something and that everyday counts. According to Pope Paul VI, "when we are born, we should be made aware that we are dying". When we have an awareness of the brevity of life, we will begin to make every moment count. It is not the duration of our lives but the lives touched by our endeavours and the impact we make on our communities, that count. It is my view that only a fraction of humanity understand this salient truth. If we spent more time thinking about the fleeting nature of life, without a doubt, we would live our lives with a sense of urgency. We would come to the sobre realisation that we will not be remembered for the things we have acquired, but for the lives we managed to touch during our brief time on earth.

"when we are born, we should be made aware that we are dying"

It is not the duration of our lives but the lives touched by our endeavours and the impact we make on our communities, that count

What difference can one person make in this world? Maybe a little, perhaps a lot, but the most important thing is that *some* difference is made. I am reminded of the story of a little girl who discovered thousands of starfish that had been washed ashore by the tidal waves. Determined to save them, she began picking them up, one at a time, and throwing them back into the ocean. An old man stood, watching her for a while. Surprised by her actions, the man walked up to her and pointed out that her efforts would hardly make a dent given the vast number of starfish stranded on the shore. Her response was remarkable, she looked up briefly before continuing her task and replied, "it might not make a difference to the lot, but I bet it makes a difference to this one". More often than not, we are paralysed by the magnitude of the problem and the fact that we are unable to make a huge difference. So, we resign ourselves to doing nothing. In the grand scheme of things, I am just one person and I may think I'm incapable of making a huge difference; but to one person, I can make a world of difference.

Man, God's Only Plan

I once heard someone say, 'God's method is man'. In other words, when God wants to do anything on earth, His preferred mode of operation is to assign a man to the task. The Bible and history books are filled with ordinary people who have made themselves available to be used by an extraordinary God. God has proven through the ages that He'll work through those who make themselves available, often bypassing those who appear more able but are less willing.

There are many heroic stories that have come out from the era of slavery and one of those that has been retold several times is that of Harriet Tubman. 'Moses', as she was later nicknamed was an unlikely candidate for the sort of feats associated with freeing more than 70 slaves. She undertook over 13 expeditions over a period of about eleven years. On the face of it, being born into slavery herself coupled with the regular seizures and migraines she suffered (the lasting effects of an injury to her head) were significant barriers to her involvement in the risky work of liberating slaves. In addition to these limitations, her small stature meant she lacked the commanding presence often associated with 'natural' leaders. Yet her deep Christian faith meant she could not turn away. She was committed to the freedom of other slaves, even at the risk of her own personal safety and freedom.

Ms.Tubman had herself escaped slavery, but repeatedly risked her life, or at the very least her freedom, in many daring exploits to see her family and other slaves also set free. It is amazing how God has programmed the human soul, such that it only finds its true rest as it helps others to find their own. Any other pursuit ultimately leads to unfulfillment; that gnawing feeling that something is missing. My belief is that this need cannot truly be satisfied by material things, but through the pursuit of a selfless life. Abraham Maslow captured this in his thesis, The Hierarchy of Needs. He identified the greatest need of man is to be significant, which he referred to as 'self actualization'. In the bible, one man is credited with, almost single-handedly, propagating the gospel beyond the Jewish nation. This is the man we know as Apostle Paul. His love for people meant he was determined that they hear the good news of Christ and know the joy he had experienced after his own unforgettable encounter with Jesus. This determination meant that he continued to spread the gospel in spite of the many beatings, deprivation and humiliating injustices he faced.

Harriet Tubman, Apostle Paul and the other examples cited in this book are not the exception, but rather the rule for how God works to impact lives and communities. I truly believe that God's strategy will not change.

This is not to say that you have to be a Christian for your life to impact others here on earth. After all, the impact made by people such as Bill Gates, founder of Microsoft, is undeniable. Through his Gates Foundation, and in collaboration with various strategic partners, Bill Gates is seeking to eradicate Malaria, endemic to the world's tropical regions. I would wager that when the history books are written, Bill and Melinda Gates will be celebrated more for their commitment to tackle malaria and poverty, than for the impressive achievements of Microsoft. There are many other examples of people who may not be as prominent as the

Gates that we all can agree, have made great impact on humanity, yet who do not even believe in God, much less an eternity with Him. However, as Christians who believe that there is more to our lives than the 'here and now' we need to be very cognisant that whatever we do has implications beyond this life.

What do you want to be remembered for?

I have had many discouraging thoughts while writing this book and have been tempted to give up on more than one occasion. The fact that I have persevered is down to a single but altogether more powerful thought, 'what if there is one person out there, whose life will be made better by the message of this book?' That possibility has made the effort and sacrifice worthwhile. What if someone was to benefit from the idea that you have carried within you for so many years? What if someone were to benefit from the time you could render in service to meet a need? What if..? What if..? Asking yourself questions like these when contemplating your projects, plans and actions will transform the way you view them.

As you read this book and ponder its message, I hope you'll be provoked to ask, 'how can I live a life that counts towards eternity?' My aspiration is that this book will impact you in ways that will count towards my eternal legacy.

CHAPTER SUMMARY

The people that make the most of their lives are those who realise that their life must count for something and that everyday counts.

It is possible to make a difference to the world even though your efforts may seem insignificant.

When God wants to do anything on earth, His preferred mode of operation is to assign a man to the task.

God works through ordinary people to do extraordinary work. He works through those who make themselves available, often bypassing those who appear more able but are less willing.

There is more to our lives than the 'here and now' and we need to be very cognisant that whatever we do has implications beyond this life.

Make it Count

What is it that you have put away and left undone for fear of failure, other seemingly valid reasons, or just sheer procrastination? Make a list of those things, no matter how insignificant or insurmountable they may seem.

CHAPTER ONE

GOD STARTS WITH ONE

Nobody can do everything, but everyone can do something. - Author Unknown

Do not let what you cannot do interfere with what you can do. - John Wooden

The LORD had said to Abram, "Go from your country, your people and your father's household to the land I will show you. - Genesis 12: 1

Studying the work of the artist Pablo Picasso, arguably one of the greatest artists of the last century, can give us an insight into his state of mind while creating these works. Similarly, taking a thoughtful look at God's creation can give us some insight into the ways that God intended the world to function.

The creation story teaches that God formed man in His own image[1] , and tasked him with procreation and the management of His creation[2] . It is not implausible to imagine an all-powerful God creating all of humanity in one go. However, in His wisdom, He decided to create one man and place within him the capacity to bring forth the rest of humanity. God put in Adam everything He wanted humanity to be. From that one man, the seven billion people that inhabit the world today emerged. Nations, cultures and races all have their source in that one man.

All through scripture, we see this model replicated in the lives of people. In an address to the nation of Israel, God drew their attention to His relationship with their ancestor, Abraham:

> "Listen to Me, you who follow after righteousness,
> You who seek the LORD: Look to the rock *from which* you were hewn, And to the hole of the pit *from which* you were dug. Look to Abraham your father, And to Sarah who bore you; For I called him alone, And blessed him and increased him" - Isaiah 51: 1 - 2.

This pattern of starting out with one man is one that is repeated over and over again in the history of the Jewish nation. The fact that God draws their attention to it (by referencing Abraham) suggests that this wasn't accidental. God's relationship with Abraham was a prototype for his relationship with them. We see this in the way the children of Israel were delivered after four hundred years of slavery. God used one man, Moses [3.] He used another man, Joshua, to lead them into their new homeland[4].

When law and order broke down, and Jewish society disintegrated into a period of chaos, it was the efforts of one woman, Deborah, that restored civility and security [5]. And when the children of Israel suffered oppression, intimidation and loss at the hands of the Midianites, an enemy nation; God used an unlikely candidate to deliver them. He used Gideon, a fearful and self-professed 'weakling' [6].

At another point in their history, while in exile, it was Mordecai's forthrightness and determination that saved them from the total annihilation orchestrated by Haman, the king's right-hand man [7]. It was a shepherd boy named David, that God used to deliver Israel from the intimidation of Goliath, and in so doing, secure the victory of the Israelites. At the time, the Israeli army was paralysed by fear; but a young lad who trusted in his God, overcame Goliath and caused the Philistine army to flee [8].

News of the broken-down wall of Jerusalem would likely have reached many of the Israelites living in captivity in the Persian empire. However, it was Nehemiah, a cup bearer in the King's palace, who decided to respond to the problem [9]. It was through a virgin, Mary, that the birth of the Messiah was realised. She believed that the unimaginable could be done through her, even though it came with the risk of being disgraced and ostracised by her community [10].

God's plan for the redemption of humanity was fulfilled through one man, Jesus Christ, the saviour of the world who came in order to die` for our sins. Our victory over sin and the devil was secured as a result of this 'one man' strategy, which was preordained by God. Jesus' death and resurrection satisfied God's righteous judgement and silenced the devil once and for all. I'll explore what this means, in further detail, in the next chapter.

Before his conversion, Saul (later known as apostle Paul) took it upon himself to intimidate believers in order to hinder the propagation of the gospel message. However, following his encounter with Christ, he became a crusader for the resurrected Lord. Paul did much to spread the gospel beyond Judea, making it accessible to many of the Roman empire. His letters to the early church based in the various Roman provinces later formed two-thirds of what is now known as the New Testament.

From Genesis through to Revelation, we see how God engages the power of one (person) to bring about the fulfilment of His divine purposes on earth. I don't believe He is about to change His way of working with humanity, in fact I believe that He wants to do the same with your life, if you let Him.

The Seed Principle

The fact that a seed has within it the potential to yield fruit not once but several times over is testament to the brilliance of God's design. All living things start life as a seed, or cell, of some sort. In the beginning, God said,

> "Let the earth bring forth grass, the herb *that* yields seed, *and* the fruit tree *that* yields fruit according to its kind, whose seed *is* in itself, on the earth; and it was so. 12 And the earth brought forth grass, the herb *that* yields seed according to its kind, and the tree *that* yields fruit, whose seed *is* in itself according to its kind."
> - Genesis 1: 11 - 12

Each and every seed has potential. Robert Schuller said, "Anyone can count the seeds in an apple, but only God can count the number of apples in a seed". When planted, an apple seed has the

"Anyone can count the seeds in an apple, but only God can count the number of apples in a seed"

potential to yield many apples which have the cumulative potential to produce an orchard of apple trees. I believe that God works with the understanding that each seed has the potential to become much greater than its current state. It requires genius such as His to see the potential in a seed.

Each individual is analogous to a seed and we all have that potential to make a difference in the lives of others and the world around us.

You have a place in God's agenda

Each of us has a unique position or part to play on earth and the world can only function optimally when each person plays his or her part. I am not a die-hard enthusiast of any particular team sport but I always find them interesting and instructive to watch. When a player is displaced, it opens the door for the opposing team to exploit. In a game of football or soccer, if a player gets sent off for any reason, his or her team is automatically at a disadvantage and becomes more vulnerable to their opponents attacks. Some teams manage to compensate for the loss, but it is often a struggle because they're playing with one less player than the opposing team. Each player has a role to play.

We are each like a piece in a giant jigsaw puzzle. As each piece finds its place, the picture becomes clearer. Each piece is part of the big picture and cannot effectively be replaced by another piece. Any attempt to do so will result in a skewed image. Each of us has a role to play in order to ensure the success of the whole.This is why the bible describes Christians as the body of Christ, with each person playing a significant role in the proper functioning of the body. [11]

Each of us has a role to play in order to ensure the success of the whole

Each of us is unique in God's creation, in other words when He made each one of us, He broke the mould. Each person's traits are a unique combination of talents and abilities. We are not accidents of nature. God had a purpose in mind when He formed you and I and gave us our particular attributes.

There are at least as many visions and ideas as there are people. Just as there are no two individuals with the same (other than identical twins) DNA, no two individuals can impact the world in exactly the same way. Some have influenced many with their unique giftings, while others have touched only a few; in both cases lives are changed. The late Steve Jobs' impact on the world is undeniable. Through the Apple brand, he harnessed creativity and technological innovation, in order to simplify and improve the productivity of millions of people.

There are also people, such as Patricia Mutsani, a member of my church, who have touched fewer lives, but no less powerfully. She brought joy back into the families of many cancer patients because she prayed with their dying loved ones and God miraculously healed them. Though she herself, had been diagnosed with terminal cancer, she managed to find the strength, compassion and faith to believe God and pray for the healing of fellow sufferers. I had the privilege of reading a letter of gratitude written by two of the ladies who were healed after Patricia prayed with them. Patricia has since received the 'all clear' from her doctors and is on the path to full recovery. Jobs and Mutsani affected people's lives in different ways, but in order to do this, both had to make a conscious decision to ensure that something or someone in the world would be made significantly better because of what they had to offer.

Don't believe the lie

One of the lies of the devil is to make us believe that our lives are not that important in the grand scheme of things and that we don't have what it takes to make a difference. I believed this lie for a long time, so much so that I subscribed to the idea that only great and famous people are able to significantly change things for the better. Such a mindset condemns one to a life of ordinariness and kills the will to try to make a difference in the lives of others. It fosters the idea that the efforts of the 'little man' do not matter to anyone, and certainly not to God.

I was deeply moved by a story I once read about a young 16th- century American missionary called David Brainerd who preached the gospel to a Native American community. During his 29 short years on earth, he only had a few converts and was not in any way famous. He never married or travelled beyond the United States, but he did record his deepest thoughts, and the events of his life and mission. His journals went on to inspire the likes of Jonathan Edwards, William Carey, John Wesley and many other prominent 18th- and 19th-century Christian missionaries and preachers. While he might have seemed unsuccessful, by many human measures of success, during his lifetime, long after his death, his life has indirectly inspired millions of people.

Brainerd's story caused me to wonder whether he lived knowing that his life's efforts mattered and whether he had an assurance that he was where God wanted him to be, doing what God wanted him to do. I wonder whether he was satisfied by the degree of success he achieved and how this compared with his own expectations and the achievements of his contemporaries. These are thoughts that I grapple with when I examine my own life. As a Christian I have come to learn that God's purpose for my life extends beyond the scope of my time here on earth, and that the choices I

God's purpose for my life extends beyond the scope of my time here on earth, and that the choices I make during my time here are significant to my eternal purpose.

make during my time here are significant to my eternal purpose. Brainerd's story introduced a new dimension to my thinking. It showed me that in addition to the eternal benefits that accrue to me by becoming more Christ-like, my life can have an earthly legacy by inspiring others, even when I am gone. It may be that I never live to see the significance of my life's efforts but I must live my life in such a way that will serve as a resource for God's glory.

God is not finished with you yet

When reading the biblical account of the life of Samson [12], it is easy to get caught up in his escapades with Delilah. These escapades teach us a lot about dealing with temptation and the importance of safeguarding against our weaknesses. However, there is another cogent lesson, which Samson's life offers us. The bible records that an Angel [13] appeared to Manoah (Samson's father) and revealed to him that he and his wife would have a son despite their prolonged infertility. The Angel went on to say that this child would have a special purpose- to initiate the deliverance from the Philistine nation.

As a man gifted with extraordinary strength, Samson, began to weaken and destroy the hold of the Philistines. Recognising his indomitable strength, the Philistines sought to look for his weakness in order to destroy him. By exploiting his weakness, they succeeded in incapacitating him. This mirrors a strategy the devil still deploys against us today.

Though Samson had been captured and shackled, he pleaded with God to be of use, one last time against the Philistines. God answered his prayer [14] and when the Philistine nobles along with their fellow countrymen gathered for a ritual celebration in honour of their god, Dagon, Samson destroyed them. In fact it is recorded that in death Samson killed more of his nation's enemies than he had during his lifetime [15]

Samson could have wallowed in his weakened and defeated state and simply accepted that it was all over, but instead, He repented of his past mistakes and asked God to strengthen him again and to give him another chance to carry out God's mandate upon his life. A preacher once said, God is not just the God of a second chance, He is the God of *another chance*. God gave Samson another chance to fulfil his life's mandate- the deliverance of Israel.

I think that when we consider Samson's life, we can be encouraged by just how little God needs. Even at our lowest ebb, if we make ourselves available, God can use us in order to make a difference, whether in life or in death. As I pondered Samson's story while writing this, the story of Claire, a hairdresser from North Kilworth, in the United Kingdom, was in the news. Claire, was a young lady who decided to raise money for the Samaritans by running in the 2012 London Marathon. Just before starting her final lap, she collapsed and died. It was such a sad turn of events. Shortly after her death, I visited the home page of her fundraising site, where she stated, "I'm running the london marathon for Samaritans because they continuously support others". She had raised about £500 prior to her death, but when the news of her death began to spread, donations skyrocketed. At the time of my writing, she had raised over £1,000,000 for the Samaritans; a charity which provides round-the-clock confidential emotional support for people who are experiencing feelings of distress or despair. Even in death, Claire's life continued to speak and positively support the work of the Samaritans as they help those in desperate need. This is not to suggest that God waits for, or facilitates our death in order to make something meaningful of our lives. The point I'm making is that His commitment to making something purposeful of our lives transcends life itself. Claire's story is on the one hand, a very sad story. Her death has no doubt left her family and loved ones bereft. On the other hand, it is also a story of an inspiring legacy.

God has started something with your life, and no matter what you have, or haven't done up to this point, God wants you to stay the course. He is determined, if you let Him, to bring about the fulfilment of His purpose in your life.

CHAPTER SUMMARY

God's strategy to achieve His divine purpose is to empower individuals that are available to be used.

Each and every person has a role to play to ensure the success of the whole team.

Even if the task before us is too large for us to complete individually, this should not prevent us from taking steps to start the task. By affecting even only a few lives (starfish) we can still making a difference to those few lives.

God is not just the God of a second chance, He is the God of *another chance*. He is always willing to give us another opportunity to make a difference.

Live life intentionally, as the impact we make in this world may outlive us.

Make it Count

Imagine your life as a seed with great potential.
What are you doing to nurture it so that it
flourishes (physically, emotionally and
spiritually)?

CHAPTER TWO

JESUS, THE ULTIMATE ONE

*All that I am I owe to Jesus Christ,
revealed to me in His divine Book.
- David Livingstone*

*You can shut him up for a fool, you can spit at him and
kill him as a demon or you can fall at his feet and call
him Lord and God, but let us not come with any
patronising nonsense about his being a great human
teacher. He has not left that open to us. He did not
intend to. - C S. Lewis*

*And there is salvation in no one else; for there is no
other name under heaven that has been given among
men by which we must be saved.
- Acts 4: 12 (NASB)*

The four gospels are an amazing body of text written by different people, but inspired by the Holy Spirit. The gospels show the different facets of the life of Jesus. Taken together they paint a picture that projects both the humanity and divinity of Jesus. Jesus, the living word of God, took on flesh and blood and dwelt amongst men.

Imagine having God, in human flesh, as your next door neighbour? It may seem unimaginable now, but over 2000 years ago, Jesus walked the streets of Jerusalem, worked as a carpenter, ate with family, friends and disciples; camped in the rough and generally lived life amongst the people in the region of Judea.

Before Jesus came in the flesh, the people relied on the Torah – God's word given through Moses- and the words of the prophets, as the ultimate guide to a holy life. The best religious teachers knew this guide by heart, but no-one could live it out fully because of the limitations of the human condition. A condition we have all inherited as a result of the fall of man in the beginning [1]. God understood that a messiah was needed to reconcile man to Himself, and a model to show him how to live. Jesus came to earth to fulfil both of these objectives.

Though Jesus was conceived supernaturally, His birth and development were as normal as that of any other child. His place of birth did not hint at his divinity, and yet His later success in public ministry could not be reconciled with his humble upbringing as a carpenter's son.

Jesus' three years of public ministry were so effective that they are still studied today by many people all over the world. Even people who do not believe in His divinity, are unlikely to dispute the effectiveness and impact of His life. One of my favourite quotes about Jesus was by Napoleon Bonaparte:

> "Alexander, Caesar, Charlemagne, and myself founded empires, but what foundation did we rest the creations of our genius? Upon force. Jesus Christ founded an empire upon love, and at this hour millions of men would die for Him."

Jesus' ministry was characterised by His service and love for all who came in contact with Him. He came as a result of love, served because of love and died out of love. His entire life on earth was orchestrated by God in heaven, in order to provide us with a model upon which to build our lives. He encapsulated this focus in a single statement

> "...even the Son of Man did not come to be served, but to serve, and to give His life a ransom for many' – Mark 10: 45

In the rest of this chapter I will explore how Jesus successfully fulfilled His mission, while on earth and what we can learn from His example.

The Plan – God's Big Idea

From our vantage point, many years after the death and resurrection of Christ, it is easier to appreciate God's plan in sending His only begotten son. In the beginning God gave Adam custody of the earth; he was to have 'dominion' over it by tending it, guarding it and generally supporting its flourishing. He lost everything because he bought the devil's lie that in instructing him and Eve not to eat of the fruit of a certain tree, God was protecting His own power rather than looking out for their interests. In other words, God couldn't be trusted and Adam had to protect his own interests. Adam allowed himself to be led down the path of disobedience rather than trust God.

The consequence of this decision was that Adam, who had been created in the likeness of God, was usurped by the devil. More tragically, he lost his intimate fellowship with God. Many of the narratives in the bible, up until Jesus' coming, are about people trying to determine their own destiny (independent of God) through their reliance on themselves or in their projection of who God is (an idol). Despite this, God kept reaching out to them but their hearts were often drawn back to the worship of their preferred gods.

Through Jesus, God showed mankind how to live in true communion with Him; and through Jesus' death for man's sins, God completed the work of restoring the severed relationship with man. He also made a way to reinstate him to his original place of dominion. Jesus' death and resurrection was God's main plan for redemption and through it, Jesus absorbed our sins into Himself, suffered the consequences of those sins and freed us from the guilt and death sentence we deserved.

His death dealt with our sin and His resurrected life has made it possible for us to overcome our sin nature.

> I have been crucified with Christ [in Him I have shared His crucifixion]; it is no longer I who live, but Christ (the Messiah) lives in me; and the life I now live in the body I live by faith in (by adherence to and reliance on and complete trust in) the Son of God, Who loved me and gave Himself up for me. - Galatians 2: 20 (Amplified)

According to God's plan now fulfilled, the resurrected Christ dwells in us, offering us the opportunity to be transformed. We are therefore no longer mere mortals, but carriers of the presence and the power of God.

I once heard the story of a man named John, a drug addict who regularly visited a certain rehabilitation programme where a Christian named Pius volunteered his time. Prior to meeting Pius, John had never before come into contact with a Christian (not that he knew that Pius was a Christian), nor had the gospel been shared with him before. However, it was evident to him that there was something different about Pius; something that distinguished him from the other volunteers. He knew that Pius attended church regularly and that on one or two occasions he shared the good news of Jesus with others within the rehabilitation programme.

Eventually, John accepted an invitation from Pius to a Church meeting. At the end of the meeting, John walked towards the altar in response to the preacher's invitation to accept Christ. At the altar, he remarked that if accepting Christ would make him like Pius, he wanted a part of it. John knew nothing about Christ, but had observed Pius who had modelled the life of Christ in the way he lived his life: loving and serving others unconditionally. What Pius progressively embodied is God's plan for all of humanity, a life that demonstrates the love of God.

We are God's dwelling place. The bible describes us as the "temple of the Holy Spirit"[2]. It was always God's plan to live in fellowship with man. That was the plan before the fall of Man and it remains the case, however it is now realised through Christ [3]. It may be difficult to comprehend, or daunting to even contemplate, that the God of all creation would choose to dwell within us. The full implication of being 'God-carriers' eludes most of us. When we look at ourselves in the mirror or look within ourselves, we don't see a superhero staring back. Quite the opposite in fact, all each of us sees is 'ordinary me'. It is amazing to think that Christ, the full expression of God on earth [4] [5] could possibly dwell in us, and that we could become an expression of His person, through living an extraordinary life for Him.

God's plan for each of us is to live a life of significance, in other words, a life that counts, and to **God's plan for** allow Christ to live within us. He **each of us is** enables the realisation of this plan by **to live a life of** helping us to serve others in love. It **significance,** was the overflow of Christ's life **in other** expressed through Pius as love and **words, a life** service that made his life attractive to **that counts** John. This is what God has in mind for us all.

His Passion

The driving force for Jesus' life was His love for God and humanity. The word 'passion' is derived from the Latin root word *passio*, which is the same word used to describe Christ's suffering on the cross. Passion is a compelling force that drives us to want to do or be something. Through the ages, no man or woman has advanced the course of humanity without being consumed by a mission. Passion is the fuel that drives the consistent pursuit of a worthwhile mission and enables one to keep going, to keep growing and to keep giving of oneself for a cause against all odds. Passion is more than just a feeling, it is rooted in conviction.

Mel Gibson's movie, *The Passion of the Christ*, paints a graphic image of what was believed to be the final twelve hours of Christ's life. I viewed the movie at the cinema and could barely watch as the actor playing Jesus Christ was beaten. My thoughts as I left the cinema were that it was near impossible for one man to go through all of that suffering. While many critics of the movie have argued that the suffering depicted in the movie was a gross exaggeration, the fact remains that Christ, who had committed no sin or criminal offence, had a passion for the salvation of the world that led Him to go through the pain and shame of the cross. The key question is, 'what would make an innocent man endure *any* suffering at all', if it could be avoided? It was His passion for humanity that made him endure the ordeal.

The Prophet Isaiah prophesied:
> "All we like sheep have gone astray; We have turned, every one, to his own way; And the LORD

has laid on Him the iniquity of us all. He was oppressed and He was afflicted, Yet He opened not His mouth; He was led as a lamb to the slaughter, And as a sheep before its shearers is silent, So He opened not His mouth. He was taken from prison and from judgment, And who will declare His generation? For He was cut off from the land of the living; For the transgressions of My people He was stricken." Isaiah 53: 6 - 8

Jesus' passion for people is evident throughout the scriptures. His words, love, service, miracles and healings were all fuelled by His passion to see the redemption of humanity and to enable man to be reconciled with God. Everything He said and did flowed out of agape love; in fact He is love personified. It was love that led him to heal the sick, meet the needs of the poor, set those held bound by life's issues and challenges free, speak up for the oppressed, proclaim the truth about the kingdom of God, raise disciples and spend time with God. It is not difficult to see where Jesus' passion lay - loving God and people.

There are only two occasions, recorded in scriptures, where Jesus wept. One was over the death of His friend Lazarus, and the second was over the city of Jerusalem. In both cases, the cause of his tears was people or communities. Jesus was in the 'people business' and that meant loving, caring, seeking the lost, meeting needs and even dying for people.

Ii is recorded that Jesus was moved with compassion when He saw the multitude of people wearied and scattered like sheep without a shepherd[6]. He was moved to respond to the pitiable state of the people. Like Jesus, we should be moved or gripped by compassion when we see spiritual or social deprivation. For some of us, it could be injustice which moves us to act, for others, it could be the effects of poverty, it might even be high teenage pregnancy rates or the plight of prisoners. Each of us must come to know what we are most passionate about. Do you know your passion?

His Priorities

Jesus' passion was dictated by God's plans, and this determined his commitments. His priorities were formed around the two things that mattered to Him the most – God and man. He lived for God, and died for humanity.

All of His thirty-three and a half years on earth were devoted to following God and serving people. At the age of twelve, the only account of Jesus' early life recorded, [7] His parents inadvertently left Him behind in Jerusalem. Once they realised He was missing, they began to search for HIm . When they eventually found Him, He seemed surprised that they had been searching for Him. He reasoned that they should have known that His priority was to do His father's

(God's) business. At the age of 12 years, Jesus was so absorbed in His discussion with the rabbis that he didn't notice his parents' absence.

We understand from the bible that Jesus spent His time with those considered sinners and outcasts. When the scribes and Pharisees saw Him in the company of social and religious outcasts they were aghast and asked His disciples, "How *is it* that He eats and drinks with tax collectors and sinners?"[8]

On hearing their question, Jesus explained that sinners, and not the righteous were His priority [9]. He spent His time eating and drinking with these social outcasts. As a result, He was called a friend of publicans and sinners [10]. If you want to know what your priorities are, consider what you spend most of your time thinking about, doing, and the things you spend most of your money on.

Jesus was not just a friend of sinners, He was also a friend of the lowly and the poor, the sick and the diseased, the lonely and the rejected, the abused and the oppressed, the widow and the fatherless. These were the people He spent most of His time with.

Mother Teresa's priority was to care for the poorest people in Calcutta, India. She remained faithful to this commitment until her death in September 1997. Even though, as a result of her work, she gained access to presidents and other world leaders, and even won a Nobel peace prize (amongst many other prizes), her focus remained caring for the poor. I believe that despite the many accolades she won, her ultimate focus was to please God.

It is evident that pleasing His Heavenly father was Jesus' priority. He strived to see every issue from God's perspective. This perspective is reflected in the way He lived His life, as recorded in scripture, and serves as an example for us. He was bound by the will of the father and that dictated His actions. His final hours in the garden of Gethsemane, before His crucifixion, were revealing. At that point, He could have chosen to prioritise His own life, but instead He chose to do the will of the Father. He was torn between living for Himself or dying to demonstrate his endless passion for God and man. He said, "No one takes it from Me, but I lay it down of Myself. I have power to lay it down, and I have power to take it again" [11]

Many times, the difficulty we face in life isn't choosing between right and wrong. Rather, it is deciding how to rank or prioritise competing good things; and then having done this, sticking with those priorities. Choosing to give to the poor out of your abundance is an obvious good thing and is easy to do, but choosing to help a friend in dire financial need when your own resources are very limited is a much more difficult choice to make. It requires a clear, prior decision to prioritise the act of giving. Further, it requires the strength to stick to that decision in the face of changing circumstances. Jesus could have chosen to continue living on earth and He had the power to do so, but He chose to lay down His life, and in so doing He aligned Himself with His two utmost priorities- God and mankind. It was a very tough choice for Him to make, so much so that the bible records that His sweat was as blood. To get through it, He sought God's help for the strength to do His will [12].

The Principles He Embodied

Principles are fundamental truths that undergird other truths. Jesus described himself as, "the way, the truth and the life" [13]. He is the Truth upon which other truths are founded. The bible contains several accounts of Jesus teaching His listeners godly principles. Jesus knew a thing or two about living a principled life. There is much we can learn from Him.

Firstly, He understood that rewards of a principled life only accrue to those who consistently apply them. He taught that anyone who lived by the principles He did, could expect to see similar, and even better, rewards. God set principles in place so that life could have generally predictable outcomes. The bible records that while the children of Israel were in the wilderness, God supernaturally provided food for them every day (Manna and quails). However, once they entered the promised land, this supernatural provision ceased [14]. He did so because He no longer wanted them to be dependent on miraculous provisions, but to apply the principle of sowing and reaping. In other words, to develop an expectation of a harvest when they planted their seeds. This forms a cycle, and for anyone willing to work hard at sowing, there is almost always a guarantee of a fruitful outcome. From that point on, when they sowed, they reaped, and if for any reason they were unable to reap, then they were to seek God's face.

Secondly, principles are fair, they work irrespective of the person applying them. Jesus said:

> "Do not judge, and you will not be judged. Do not condemn, and you will not be condemned. Forgive, and you will be forgiven. Give and it will be given to you. A good measure, pressed down, shaken together and running over, will be poured into your lap. For with the measure you use, it will be measured to you" - Luke 6: 37- 38.

The applicability of these principles is not limited only to His disciples and other listeners at that time; He was laying out divinely ordained universal principles. They are applicable to our lives today.

Supernatural Power

Many times in scripture, and as explored in the preceding section, Jesus affirmed certain principles, but in some cases, He overruled earthly principles. This shows that while the invincible God institutes earthly principles, He is not constrained by them. The miracle of Jesus walking on water, recorded in the gospels, taught His disciples a lesson on faith and the power of God. By walking on water, He defied a law of physics, articulated two hundred years before by the Greek mathematician Archimedes, about the buoyancy of objects immersed in liquids.

Power is the ability to effect change. Jesus came to bring about change. Circumstances never fazed Him because He always saw things God's way and was able to tap into heaven's power in any matter. A wise man once remarked that, "when you have seen the magnitude of God, everything else pales into nothingness". Jesus was well aware of this. Time and again, both in the old and new Testaments in the bible, we read of miracles in which God's will took precedence over the laws of nature. When we, as God's people call on Him in the midst of impossible situations, He is able to break through and help us- in many cases, miraculously. Miracles happen when God steps into our situation in order to bring us out of it. It is God's way of saying that while He has put principles in place to guide human life on earth, He is able to displace or suspend the normal order of things.

Jesus needed power from heaven to fulfil His earthly ministry, we too need power from heaven to do the work of Heaven here on earth. He executed His ministry through the power of the Holy Spirit; God's enabling power on earth. The bible informs us that, "God anointed Jesus of Nazareth with the Holy Spirit and with power, who went about doing good and healing all who were oppressed by the devil, for God was with Him"[15]. The purpose of this power is to enable us do good and to bring about relief from all forms of oppression, both in our lives and those of others.

During His time on earth Christ often demonstrated access to supernatural power. As Christians, our relationship with God means that we have access to that same supernatural power.

The Precedent-setter

In our world today, it is very difficult to find a role model worthy of emulation. Jesus Christ did not only come to earth to die for our sins, He came to show us how to live. Although, crucified over 2000 years ago, the way He lived His life remains applicable today.

In my first book, *Leading the Right Side Up*, I wrote about Jesus' approach to leadership and how His example radically changed my understanding of who a leader is. He asked His disciples, "For who is greater, he who sits at the table, or he who serves? Is it not he who sits at the table?'... 'Yet I am among you as the One who serves"[16]. He taught leadership through serving others, loving through giving, and living through obedience.

Jesus washed the feet of His disciples; a very humble act of service. In those days, it was a task carried out by the lowliest household servant. His clear message to his disciples, then and today, was that since He as our Lord and teacher, was willing to wash the feet of His disciples as an act of service, we should be willing to serve one another in whatever way necessary. He demonstrated the greatest love by giving His life for us; He observed, "there is no greater love than for a man to give his life for that of His friends"[17]. He gave us the gift of life, so that all men could have access to eternal life. Love is a demanding practice, yet, it is in giving it that we find true fulfilment. In his book, The *Mystery of Marriage*, Mike Mason made a thought-

"love asks for everything. Not just a little bit, or a whole lot, but for everything. And unless one is challenged to give everything, one is not really in love"

provoking statement about the characteristics of love, "love asks for everything. Not just a little bit, or a whole lot, but for everything. And unless one is challenged to give everything, one is not really in love" [18]. Jesus demonstrated this by giving His life (everything) for all, and while most of us will not have to lay down our physical lives, we should expect that love towards others will demand a lot from us.

Jesus also modelled total obedience to God. He lived it out- even to the point of death on the cross [19]. As a result of submitting to God in full unreserved obedience, God exalted Him and gave Him "a name above all other names" [20]. For Him, obedience to God was a delight. The psalmist captured the radical obedience to God that would characterise the life of Jesus when he prophesied, "Sacrifice and offering You did not desire; My ears You have opened. Burnt offering and sin offering You did not require. Then I said, "Behold, I come: In the scroll of the book it is written of me. I delight to do your will, O my God, and your law is within my heart"[21]. Obedience to God is at the core of true discipleship and it is a price that every follower of Christ must learn to pay. Jesus, therefore did not merely ask us to obey, but has shown us through His own life what obedience to God really looks like.

The Price

When I think of the price God paid for my redemption by giving His only begotten son to die on the cross for my sake, it reassures me of my worth to God and offers me a sense of personal value. No one pays for junk. In His death, Jesus paid the ultimate price for our souls; the guiltless for the guilty. Scripture records that the price we ought to pay for our sin is death (eternal separation from God), but Jesus paid the price instead. He sacrificed His life so that through His death, God could justify our redemption.

> "For the wages of sin is death, but the gift of God is eternal life in Christ Jesus" - Romans 6:23.

When I think of the price God paid for my redemption by giving His only begotten son to die on the cross for my sake, it reassures me of my worth to God and offers me a sense of personal value. No one pays for junk.

In ancient times, people sacrificed animals in order to be cleansed from their sins. These sacrifices had to be continual as they fell so short of what was required for full atonement of man's propensity for sin. They were a foreshadow of the ultimate sacrifice that Christ would eventually make. By the singular event of His death and resurrection, all our sins were remitted and we were given a new lease of life, once and for all[22]. Praise the Lord!!

In chapter one, I wrote about the 'seed principle' and explained its parallels with Jesus' life on earth. The bible teaches that unless a grain of wheat falls to the ground and dies, it abides alone [23], it is only through its death (by germinating) that it brings forth much fruit. Through Jesus' sacrificial death, God made a way for the salvation of the souls of all men who accept the sacrifice. To Him, the reward makes the price paid worth it.

Anyone who desires to live a life that counts needs to be aware that there is a price to pay. In a sense, it will often require living a sacrificial life – denying yourself certain things to focus on the needs of a cause. Jesus' obedience, even to death, earned Him a name above all names [24]. Surely, one would have thought that there must be another way to glory, but even Jesus had to pay a price. I learnt long ago that there is a price for everything I desire to have. Everything carries a price tag, and we should all learn to ask what the cost is. After all, no one walks into a car showroom and drives off in a brand new car without having put in the effort to organise their finances, nor do we go into a supermarket and load up our shopping trolleys without ensuring we have sufficient funds to cover the cost of the items. Even if payment is waived and we get these things for 'free', we must realise that someone else paid the price for it.

In a letter to his protégé, Timothy, apostle Paul wrote,

> "For I am already being poured out as a drink
> offering, and the time of my departure is at hand.
> I have fought the good fight, I have finished the
> race, I have kept the faith. Finally, there is laid up
> for me the crown of righteousness, which the Lord,
> the righteous Judge, will give to me on that Day,
> and not to me only but also to all who have loved
> His appearing." - 2 Timothy 4: 6 - 8

In this valedictory note, it was clear that he had finished his
leg of the race and was ready to pass the baton on to the
next generation of Christian leaders. He had paid the price,
now he longed for the prize.

His Programme

Jesus came to fulfil the prophecy given by the prophet
Isaiah,

> "The Spirit of the Lord God is upon Me, Because
> He has anointed Me to preach good tidings to the
> poor; He has sent Me to heal the broken-hearted,
> To proclaim liberty to the captives and recovery of
> sight to the blind, To set at liberty those who are

oppressed; to proclaim the acceptable year of the
Lord" - Isaiah 61: 1 – 2

He used this scripture to set out His manifesto on earth[25].
After reciting the prophecy in the temple, He declared
boldly, to all who were present that the scripture was
fulfilled in their hearing. He explained that He had come to:
Preach the good news to the poor: The word 'poor' covers
various classes of poverty, including material poverty (such
as those who lack daily sustenance); spiritual poverty (those
who lack the eternal assurance of salvation); and physical
poverty (those who lack of physical wellbeing or health in
their body - the sick).

Heal the broken-hearted: Those who have suffered
emotional trauma and have been left feeling rejected,
disappointed, or despondent.

Bring liberty to the captives: Those who are unlawfully held
bound in such a way that their progress is hindered by some
form of oppression (demonic) or physical incarceration.

Affect the recovery of sight to the blind: This category
included both those who were physically blind and those
who were spiritually blind i.e. unable to accurately discern
their own spiritual state.

Grant liberty to the oppressed: those who by reason of fear or manipulation are being abused or enslaved.

Jesus went about fulfilling the mandate entrusted to Him by His father and in three and a half years, He managed to achieve a whole lot more than any other human being on earth.

CHAPTER SUMMARY
There is a price to pay if you want to live a life that counts - make a difference in the world. Jesus paid the ultimate price.

As believers, our lives are not our own. Jesus' life was characterised by his love and service for all who came into contact with Him.

Jesus affirmed certain principles, but in some cases, He overruled them. This shows that while the invincible God institutes earthly principles, He is not constrained by them.

By modelling our lives on Jesus, the Holy Spirit will empower us to impact others.

Obedience to the Holy Spirit's direction within us will help us line up our passions, purpose, service and conviction with those of God.

Make it Count

What five things about Jesus' life do you find most inspiring? How can these be fully expressed in your own life?

CHAPTER THREE

ONE CAN MAKE A DIFFERENCE

To the world you may be one person,
But to one person you may be the world.
- Anonymous

If you think you are too small to make a difference,
you have never been in bed with a mosquito.
- Betty Reese

Then the LORD turned to him and said,
"Go in this might of yours, and you shall save Israel
from the hand of the Midianites. Have I not sent you?"
...And the LORD said to him, "Surely I will be with you,
and you shall defeat the Midianites as one man."
- Judges 6: 14, 16

A few years ago whilst in Ukraine on a ministry programme, I told a fellow attendee about the idea for this book. During our discussion, he offered me a copy of the poem below as potential material for the book:

> **I am only one;**
> **But still I am one**
> **I cannot do everything;**
> **But still I can do something**
> **And because I cannot do everything;**
> **I will not refuse to do something that I can do**
> - Edward Everret Hale

I like this poem because while it acknowledges the limitations of the individual, it does not suggest that they're an excuse for inaction. It makes the point that while none of us will be able to do everything, this recognition should not be allowed to render us so discouraged that we do nothing at all.

As a student of life and a keen observer of people, I've come to believe that the difference between those who continue to do things in ordinary ways and those who venture into more innovative or radical approaches and achieve extraordinary results is mainly about perspective. Those that truly make a difference usually have the understanding that whatever they do, no matter how small, makes a difference in the grand scheme of things.

A popular story about three builders who were hired to construct a building helps illustrate this point. All three builders had seen the plans before setting to work. When the first was asked what he was doing, he replied 'I am laying bricks'. In response to the same question, the second answered, 'I am working on a building'; but the third builder, with much excitement in his voice, stated, 'I am building a cathedral'. The three men were doing similar things, but saw their work differently. The first bricklayer came to work simply to lay bricks, and did not

Those that truly make a difference usually have the understanding that whatever they do, no matter how small, makes a difference in the grand scheme of things

think that what he was doing made a significant difference. The second bricklayer saw a bit further, but not far enough to see the full impact of the work he was doing. However, the third bricklayer knew he was playing a key part in something much bigger than himself. I imagine his attitude affected his work.

I think many of us are like the first two bricklayers - we've bought into the lie that that we don't matter much and neither does the work we do. This doesn't negate the old saying that two heads are better than one, all I'm saying is that an individual can do great things and make a difference without necessarily having to wait for a partner or team. However, only those who've broken free of the spell of this lie are truly able to harness this 'power of one'.

I must stress that I am not advocating individualism, but rather the recognition of each individual's potential within a community. It is this recognition that leads to individuals taking responsibility for events happening around them and engenders participation in community.

I used to believe that my actions, did not make much of a difference. For many years this perspective prevented me from striving to achieve anything significant. The truth of the matter is that if you don't believe that your individual contributions make a difference to the work of a team, you are likely to believe that you are insignificant even if the team is successful.

When training volunteers at our church, I often try to stress that not everyone can be the pastor, but every one of us has a role to play. How we choose to play this role can have a positive or detrimental effect on others. I remember a church member who stopped attending church services for a while because of the manner in which a church usher addressed her. She took offence, returned home and stopped attending church for a while. The way that usher chose to play his role had the effect of turning a regular member back home, costing her the opportunity to hear the choir minister in song, the sermon, as well as the chance to commune with other Christians in collective worship. This illustrates the power of the individual to make an impact on other people, by how he or she chooses to act.

God created each one of us, and infused us with His life. We each express His life within us in different ways, such that each of us is able to make a contribution for the greater good. In other words, no two people can offer exactly the same thing; each person is **act knowing that what we offer makes a difference, because it does.** unique. With this in mind, it is then important that we act knowing that what we offer makes a difference, because it does.

I suspect that people who seem content to stand back and do nothing sincerely believe that nothing they do will make a difference; but I'm firm in my conviction that nothing could be further from the truth.

Little things can make a big difference
Everyday, people overlook small opportunities to make a difference in their jobs, in the lives of colleagues, in their communities, and with their families and friends. Many times, it's the little things that we do that make a big

difference. Being genuinely interested in a colleague's well-being or standing up for the oppressed in our communities may seem inconsequential but makes a difference to those concerned. The impact of a teacher, who takes the time to speak words of affirmation to a child whose self-esteem is continually being degraded at home, may seem a small thing. However, those words might be a lifeline for such a child. According to Sydney Smith, a writer and Anglican cleric, "it is the greatest of all mistakes to do nothing because you can only do little. Do what you can". I think these are important words to remember. Otherwise, the enormity of the tasks or problems we face will push us to throw up our hands and do nothing, reasoning that our efforts would be no more than a drop in the proverbial ocean.

The biblical parable of the servants who were given 'talents', or 'investment capital' in today's parlance, by their master and instructed to invest and generate a profit, teaches us a lot about stewardship [1]. The two servants who were given larger amounts to invest made a profit, but the servant who had been given the least investment capital, chose not to invest it at all and simply returned it to his master upon the latter's return. This third servant may have thought that his actions were justified. He did not appear to have seriously considered the option of investing the capital. Perhaps he was preoccupied with thoughts of what he might have been able to do with more investment capital. If so, I would suggest that he might have been better served by thinking that even a small investment was better than having nothing at all. After all, it's possible to make a return even on a small investment.

Our little becomes much when we place it in the hands of the master

Jesus wanted to feed the several thousand people that had gathered to hear Him speak[2]. The scale of the need paralysed the disciples from making any real effort to address it, and as a result they suggested that Jesus should send them away to fend for themselves. The only food that could be found was five barley loaves and two small fish - a young boy's packed lunch. Andrew, one of Jesus' disciples was quick to point out that the packed lunch was insignificant in comparison to the needs of the crowd that they were looking to feed. But Jesus wanted to show them (and us) that God intervenes when we take our little and put it in His hands. Jesus blessed the little boy's lunch and miraculously, all the people ate to satisfaction and there were even leftovers. The main lesson of this story is that when, we take responsibility for alleviating the need we see around us, and refuse to be discouraged by our lack of resources, God intervenes in our cause.

Mother Teresa understood how daunting it could be to face an enormous task without possessing the necessary resources to address the challenge but she said, "If you can't feed a hundred people, then feed just one". She would not allow her limited resources to paralyse her efforts. In her work with the very poor in India, she was confronted by the dire needs of people on a daily basis and was often unable to solve the entire problem. That didn't stop her from doing her best. Despite her meagre resources, she was able to help thousands of people find dignity and peace even in their final hours. Today, missionaries from the organisation she founded are in many nations around the world. All because a petite nun with a huge heart refused to allow her limitations stop her helping people.

Whoever has, to him more will be given

One of my favourite sayings of Jesus is, "for whoever has, to him more will be given, and he will have abundance; but whoever does not have, even what he has will be taken away from him" [3]. When I came to understand this text, it changed my perspective on life quite considerably. Jesus is communicating a truth, which to a large extent underpins success and the distribution of resources. Everyone has 'something'. You may not have what you want, but what you have is often able to get you what you want. Often times, when we make statements such as, 'I have nothing', or 'I cannot do anything', we undermine what we have and so we shut ourselves off from God's providence. Jesus was teaching here that to those who believe that they have something to offer and act accordingly, God makes more resources available. I learnt this principle at a time when I was going through what I have described as a prolonged 'valley experience'. I had no money, and to make matters worse, no job. It was a rather depressing time for someone like me who thrives on being productive.

At first, during this period, I did not give an offering in church because I did not think I had any money to give, but one day, while I was studying the bible I came upon these words of Jesus. As a result I saw my situation in a new light and from that point I refused to accept that I had nothing to give. Following the revelation, I searched my room and found a jar of pennies that I had collected over the years. Every Sunday from that point on, I would give an offering in church of ten copper coins. Although I was embarrassed to give such a small amount, I kept on giving. My perspective changed and I saw myself as someone who had something to offer. I no longer see situations as insurmountable. I understand that I might not be able to do everything or change everything, but one thing is guaranteed, I will play my part rather than throw up my hands in frustration or walk away for fear of not being able to make a big difference.

All it takes is one person

The Arab spring was triggered by the actions of a young Tunisian man, who was no longer able to bear the injustice and oppression that was prevalent in his nation. That young man was a street vendor called Mohamed Bouazizi. On the 17th of December 2010 he decided to set himself alight in protest at the confiscation of his wares and the subsequent harassment and humiliation inflicted on him by a municipal official and her aides. His action triggered a revolution that eventually spread across the Middle East and caught the attention of the world.

John Wesley is quoted as saying, 'Catch on fire with enthusiasm and people will come for miles to watch you burn.' Wesley didn't intend for his words to be taken literally and was in no way promoting extremism; he was simply pointing out that people who are enthusiastic and passionate about the cause they seek to advance tend to capture other people's attention. The sad event described above caught the attention of the world because one person who was tired of the situation he was in, decided to act. Using the only thing he felt he had left, his body, he decided to make a statement to the whole world.

John the Baptist was tucked away in the desert. He was one man, crying out in the wilderness, and yet many from the cities thronged to him to hear his firebrand message. At a time when there was no email, Twitter or mobile communication, his message of repentance and baptism spread through every level of society. He was the most unlikely candidate to attract a crowd of people. His diet and sense of style were unconventional, to say the least.

Inspite of this he managed to capture the hearts and minds of the people. Unfortunately, many of us are not enthusiastic about the lives we have been given or the mission we are called to. We have been assigned on to His majesty's service, our life and mission are important enough to make a difference. This is not so much because of us, but because of the one who has commissioned us. God is looking for people who will rise from being complacent and recognise that though they might not have much in the material sense, they have all they need to make a statement for God to the world.

The Centurion Made a Difference

When the centurion heard that Jesus was coming to town, he asked the elders of the city to request that Jesus, visit his home to heal one of his servants. The elders pleaded with Jesus to visit the centurion's home saying, "for he loves our nation, and he is the one who built us our synagogue." [4]The good deeds of this centurion commended him to men.

In this story, the Centurion epitomised a life that made a difference in the lives of other people. This is especially remarkable when one considers that the relationship between heathen Roman soldiers and the local Jewish population in Judea and Galilee at the time, was hardly amicable. Certainly, it was rare for a centurion to be so invested in the Jewish community as to build them a synagogue. In their plea, the Jewish elders stressed that the centurion was deserving of a blessing because of his love of the Jewish nation as demonstrated by his construction of a synagogue. It is also noteworthy that his appeal to Jesus was not for the healing of his own son or daughter, but of his servant.

I believe Jesus took interest in this case for two reasons: the value the centurion placed on the life of his servant and the testimony of the elders. Whenever I read this scripture, I wonder whether people will speak about my love for and goodwill towards the people in my community.

Evil prevails when good people do nothing

Have you ever wondered why certain spheres are dominated by people who don't necessarily have society's best interests at heart? A glaring example is the arena of politics where some people vie for political office with a barely disguised desire for personal enrichment or some other self-serving agenda. When this happens, we may sit back and moan about how displeased we are about it, but that is often where it ends. The truth of the matter is that, because nature abhors a vacuum, if well-meaning and competent people do not rise up to the task, those with negative ulterior motives will keep gaining ground. It is true that 'all it takes for evil to prevail is for good people to stand back and do nothing'. All it takes to dispel abject darkness in a room is to light a candle. You and I are called to be that light in our own world and as we allow our 'little' light to shine, we are able to push back the encroaching darkness.

All it takes to dispel abject darkness in a room is to light a candle. You and I are called to be that light in our own world

CHAPTER SUMMARY

One person may not have the power or opportunity to do everything but the little effort he or she contributes makes a difference.

We should not be dismissive of the little we have. Every gift, talent and ability we have counts, nothing is too little.

God can and will supplement our ordinary ability with His supernatural power when we make ourselves available for His purposes.

We should use our gifts to do what we can now instead of waiting for more money, a more developed talent etc.

If we do not rise up to the task, those with negative ulterior motives will.

Make it Count

Oftentimes, we make complaints about things we are not satisfied with, but hardly make an effort to try and change it. What is it that you find most deplorable, and what will you do in order to try and make a difference in that area?

CHAPTER FOUR

THE IMPACT OF ONE

*Each day when I awake I know I have one more day to
make a difference in someone's life"*
- James Mann

Instead of counting your days, make your days count.
- Anonymous

*A little one shall become a thousand and a small one a
strong nation. I, the Lord, will hasten it in its time.*
- Isaiah 60: 22

E very significant change in my life has been effected
through a person. Several years back, I was stuck in
very uncomfortable and dilapidated accommodation.
It was a very disheartening experience. At the time, I lived

in a rundown three-bedroom house with two other housemates as well as my younger sister, with whom I shared a room. The house was mice-infested and the toilet broke down regularly, often for weeks at a time. It was so bad that I felt depressed at the thought of going home, and having friends and family over was something I had come to loathe. We weren't in a position to press the landlord to deal with the problems because over the course of a year, we had racked up over £10,000 debt in rent arrears, due in part to unemployment and an unprofitable business venture. I then started a job and became desperate to move. At this point I met a gentleman who became a mentor to me and challenged me to break out of my current situation by taking a leap of faith and renting a three-bedroom apartment in a better part of town. Covering the rent would have stretched my finances too far for comfort but my mentor encouraged me to think creatively. So, in an agreement with my new landlord, I decided to sublet the third bedroom which enabled me to comfortably pay the rent on the new apartment. I now had a room to myself as did my sister.

Things have moved on since then, but I will never forget what this person did for me and more so the lessons I learnt through that experience. It is one for which I am eternally grateful. I could share many other experiences and I am sure as you read this, you can probably think of experiences in your life where you were impacted by the unselfish act of others.

The value of one

In life there are people, who add value to us, and others whose interactions with us have a diminishing effect. Every time we come in contact with people, we impact their lives, whether positively or negatively. Each event or relational experience leaves an impact, some which are easily forgotten, and others which are more difficult to forget. As we come into relationships, we each come with our offering, which in itself has inherent value.

For over a decade now, my aspiration has been to add value to those I come in contact with. I am not implying in any way that there is a lack of value in those people I seek to help. All I am trying to do is unveil the inherent value that the almighty God placed in each and everyone of His creation and by so doing, add something of value to such a life. This has to be the case, because God never makes junk nor did He send His son to die for worthless entities. When God made man in the beginning, He looked at him and declared him, "very good"[1] .

Neither I, nor the people I come into contact with are worthless. God took time to form me and lavished me with gifts and abilities, so that I could share these with others in a way that is beneficial to them. For many years, I took my individual gifts and abilities for granted, I considered them

my assignment in life is to share my gifts and the benefit of these experiences with those I come in contact with.

to be common-place. But this simply isn't true; these attributes, and the way I use them, make me unique. This applies to every other human being too. My life experiences are not commonplace, they are particular to me. The person I am is a composite of my experiences, and my assignment in life is to share my gifts and the benefit of these experiences with those I come in contact with.

The average person has many different skills and abilities, most of which will remain dormant. Are there giftings and abilities that you previously identified in yourself but subsequently considered to be insignificant or unworthy of further exploration and so, discarded? Perhaps, while growing up you were not encouraged to develop such skills or weren't taught how valuable they could be. I suspect that many people are able to think of at least a few talents or nascent skills that they discarded because they seemed unimportant. Oftentimes, not being able to see value in what we have affects our general outlook in life and can result in a low opinion of self. As long as this perspective remains, our ability to add value will be greatly diminished. But if we know that we have what it takes to make a difference, we are more inclined to see the value of our efforts and derive a sense of fulfilment from them. In his letter to the Corinthian Church, Paul admonished them saying:

"throw yourselves into the work of the Master, confident that nothing you do for him is a waste of time or effort." - 1 Corinthians 15: 58b (Message).

Sadly, some of the people that have made the greatest impact on my life are unaware of how much of a blessing they have been to me. These people often deflect my gratitude for their actions. They do not really see their contributions as significant. For many years, I too struggled to believe the compliments paid to me by those I'd worked closely with. This wasn't

Humility is important but we should also learn to accept and appreciate the value that God has placed in each of us.

down to false humility, I simply found such compliments hard to believe. Humility is important but we should also learn to accept and appreciate the value that God has placed in each of us. Now, with a much better sense of my own value I have more confidence. I approach all that I do with the understanding that my efforts, however little, can make a difference. Incidentally, this confidence has the effect of drawing out the confidence of others too. I am also less threatened by other people because I have a quiet appreciation of the value that I am able to add to the lives of others.

When my son was a baby he had a bib inscribed with the words 'A person is very important, no matter how small'. It always made me smile. Whenever he had it on, I'd think, 'he's demanding [albeit it, without being aware of it] to be treated with respect'. Despite his small stature, God has placed within him, value that will manifest in time. The book of Matthew describes how Jesus had to intervene in an argument that erupted amongst His disciples[2]. The disciples were arguing about the characteristics of the greatest person in the kingdom of heaven. To illustrate His point, Jesus gently pulled out a little child from amongst the gathered crowd. He explained that the greatest in the Kingdom of heaven is one who has the characteristics and outlook of a little child. Later in the same chapter, He teaches His disciples a very important lesson about the value the Kingdom of God places on every single person. He used a parable about a sheep-owner's reaction to the loss of a single sheep to illustrate His point. Jesus pointed out that if a sheep-owner lost one of a hundred sheep, he would leave the ninety-nine and go looking for the one stray sheep. Jesus explained that this behaviour mirrored that of God's. The implication was that a single lost sheep is as important as ninety-nine safe ones and that God feels the same way about lost people [3]. Whenever I read this text, I find the suggestion that the missing one is equivalent to the remaining ninety-nine, both baffling and wondrous. Baffling because surely, one sheep cannot be equivalent in value to ninety-nine others. The kingdom of Heaven's outlook is the very antithesis of our modern, utilitarian perspective. I find it wondrous because what Jesus is saying here is that God works to prevent the loss of anything of value to Him, however small it may seem in the grand scheme of things. Regardless of the breadth and depth of his great wealth, His heart is fixed on seeking out the one that is lost.

Ways to Impact

Assuming you are now, or have always been, convinced of the importance of making an impact through your unique gifts and talents, you may be thinking, 'yes, but *how* can I make an impact?' Well, there are several ways, but I have grouped them into five broad categories:

The Words We Speak

Words of affirmation and encouragement can have such a strong impact that their effects can last a lifetime. The affirming words of a parent, teacher, or some other authority figure have been known to significantly impact lives. Words can be carriers of blessings and by the same token, of curses. The bible records that just before his death, Jacob gathered his sons together and 'spoke into their lives'. To his first-born son, Reuben, he said,

> "Reuben, you are my firstborn, my might and the beginning of my strength, the excellency of dignity and the excellency of power. Unstable as water, you

shall not excel, because you went up to your father's
bed; then you defiled *it* ...— Genesis 49: 3-4.

Reuben's unruly sexual appetite had led him to commit a
sexual act with his father's concubine, Bilhah. Reuben was
Jacob's firstborn son and was entitled to a significant
inheritance by virtue of this, unfortunately his
dishonourable actions earned him a curse instead. The curse
Jacob pronounced over Reuben reverberated through many
generations of Reuben's lineage.

God's affirmation of Jesus as His beloved son at His
baptism reassured Jesus and propelled Him into the world-
changing ministry (service) that took up the next three years
of His life.

"And suddenly a voice came from heaven, saying,
"This is My beloved Son, in whom I am well
pleased" Matthew 3: 17.

During my teenage years, one of my older siblings
repeatedly told me that I was lazy. There was some truth to
this, as like many teenagers, I had a habit of lazing about
the house. Unfortunately, his words had such an impact on
me, that to this day, well beyond my teenage years, I still
have the sneaky feeling that I *am* lazy. Most times, I manage
to turn the negative emotions that accompany this feeling

around by using it to challenge myself to greater things but occasionally, this result in overwork. I know people who were told by their fathers that they would never succeed in life, and many of them are still struggling to overcome the low self-esteem that those words engendered.

Long ago, before I developed an appreciation for the power of words, I used them carelessly as well, and my younger sister often bore the brunt of this. I now regret making careless remarks that inflicted emotional bruises on her and others. A lady I knew once told me that whenever she saw me approaching she would deliberately change course in order to avoid me as she was fearful of what I might say to her. When I heard this, I felt terribly bad and asked God to help me deal with this. Thankfully, He did. My father, on the other hand was, and still is, a man with a deep understanding of the power of words. He was always very careful about what he said to his children. This is even more the case now that he's older. I always look forward to my chats with him because our conversations always end with him pronouncing blessings over my life. I have since learnt that power lies in the words that we speak and I am now a lot more cautious about what I say.

Too often we underestimate the power of a kind word, an honest compliment, or an accurate criticism made in love; all of which have the potential to turn a life around. The

words that we speak have great impact. They can be
affirmative and help to build up people's self-belief and
confidence. They can also be encouraging and help people
to keep going. Our words have the power to help people
assess and realign their behaviour or to envision and work
towards a better future.

The warmth we create

A warm attitude always makes a positive impression on its
beneficiaries, but creating and maintaining this atmosphere
of warmth requires deliberate effort. If you desire to have an
impact on other people, a warm and friendly attitude is
necessary. Think of the friends or colleagues who are just
great to have around. Isn't it their attitude and the way that
they make you feel that draws you to them? They tend to be
non-judgemental and generally relaxed in their attitude to
life. Now ask yourself whether others want to be around
you? For some, being warm and friendly is easy because of
their natural disposition. For me however, it requires
conscious effort. I do not always get it right, but when I do,
the positive effects I see spur me on. The fact that so many
people regularly flocked to hear Jesus' sermons
demonstrates how much people liked being around Him.
This was because they could sense that He genuinely valued
people and so, they were drawn to Him.

Jesus demonstrated that it is possible to love and be at ease with people whilst leading them. His behaviour was in sharp contrast to the stiff and judgemental manner the Pharisees and Sadducees (who made up the religious establishment of the day) tended to adopt. They sought to ensure adherence to the law by instilling fear in the people and tended to maintain some distance from them. The difference is that Jesus valued people and was always looking for ways to add value. The inevitable result was an atmosphere that was both warm and welcoming. And that's the secret of relational impact- learning to value people.

The work we do

Work always provides us with an opportunity to impact others. This is true whether it is paid employment or done on a voluntary basis. The attitude we adopt while working and the extent to which we help others through our work determines the level of our impact. As I touched on earlier in this book, our perception of the work we do colours the way we do it. If our work represents nothing more than a means to earn a living, then I contend that our impact levels will be very low.

Martin Luther King Jnr once said, "If a man is called to be a street sweeper, he should sweep streets even as Michelangelo painted, or Beethoven composed music, or Shakespeare wrote poetry. He should sweep streets so well that all the hosts of heaven and earth will pause to say, here

lived a great street sweeper who did his job well." Martin
Luther King Jnr understood the importance of perspective.
He also recognised that the level of impact a person's work
can have on society is not a function of the type of work
they do. His life's work bore witness to this understanding.
As a preacher he sought to liberate the souls of men but he
also applied himself to securing civil liberties for an
oppressed people. Through his work, he impacted millions.
Today, many people still celebrate the contribution of
Martin Luther King Jnr.

The wealth we share

There is an old saying: 'the best things in life are free'.
There is some truth to this. Serving others does not
necessarily carry a hefty price tag but a lack of resources
can get in the way of us making a significant impact. The
bible encourages us to provide food for the famished soul.
So, if a man is hungry, words are not enough. We ought to
go further. In fact the bible tells us that when we meet the
practical needs of people in this way, it is as though we do
it unto Jesus Himself.

> "For I was hungry and you gave Me food; I was
> thirsty and you gave Me drink; I was a stranger and
> you took Me in" - Matthew 25: 35.

Providing practical support requires **Time is one of** resources. It's important to point out **the most** that by 'resources' I'm not referring **important** solely to money. Time is one of the **resources we** most important resources we have. It is **have** possible to work to make back any money you give away but this is not the case with our time. Once it is gone, time can never be regained. Often times, when we neglect the needs of others, it's because we're reluctant to devote the time required to address them. The parable of the good Samaritan sets out how one man went out of his way to help a man who had been robbed, wounded and left half-dead. The religious folks who ought to have helped, saw the injured man but crossed to the other side of the road and continued on their journeys. The Samaritan, who was under no religious or cultural obligation to do so, stopped to help. He allowed his schedule to be interrupted because he valued the human life in front of him over his schedule. He expended his time and money to see that the man was tended to. There are many possible reasons why the priest and the Levite passed by without stopping and many bible scholars and teachers have speculated about what these might be. I think one of the most important insights we can draw from this parable is that there's a cost to loving one's neighbour. In other words, we should expect to expend our resources and be aware that, often times, loving our neighbours will be inconvenient.

Our witness to others

A witness is someone who shares a story or provides evidence of what he or she has seen or experienced. Every Christian is called to be a witness of Christ to others. In fact the Holy Spirit was given to all who believe in the lordship of the resurrected Christ in order that we may bear witness of Him. Many Christians reduce the work of the Holy Spirit to the endowment of the prayer language of 'tongues' or simply being the enabler of God's blessings. Actually the primary function of the Holy Spirit is to equip and enable the believer to become true witnesses for Christ [4].

Being a witness is not just about what we say, it is also about who we are. Jesus Christ came as a witness of the Father. On one occasion, He said to His disciples, if you have seen me, then you have seen the Father. I have always sought to be a true witness of who Jesus is and His mission on earth, through the way I lead my life. St Francis of Assisi said, "Preach the gospel at all times and when necessary use words."

Every Christian is called to be a witness and we are afforded opportunities to do so as we go about the daily business of living our lives. I have read and heard many stories about people who have done this well but the story of Patricia Mutsani, which I shared in chapter one of this book, is particularly striking. While coming to terms with her own seemingly hopeless situation, she reached out to several other women in the same hospital, who were in a similar situation. She would pray with them and in time, she saw them totally healed of cancer, and more importantly, she shared the gospel with them. She continued to do this even while was dealing with her own pain. No-one would have blamed her for being preoccupied with her own life-threatening medical issues. However because she understood that God could use her as a witness for Him, she chose to be one.

Different levels of Impact

Jesus intimated that He viewed the things we do to help others as help rendered to Him[5]. He listed a few specific examples such as feeding and clothing the poor, and visiting the sick and incarcerated but there are many more things that we can do to help others. For example, we could adopt or sponsor a child that is in straitened circumstances, we could care for victims of rape or fight to stop injustice in war-ravaged countries, to mention a few. All our actions aimed at bringing about the good of others matter to Jesus, regardless of the scale of the impact.

Former American President, Jimmy Carter said, "I have one life and one chance to make it count for something . . . Now, my faith goes beyond theology and religion and requires considerable work and effort. My faith demands — this is not optional — my faith demands that I do whatever I can, wherever I am, whenever I can, for as long as I can with whatever I have to try to make a difference."

As a Christian, President Jimmy Carter demonstrated his faith by seeking to impact nations and people in different ways. His mantra is one that should be adopted by every believer in Christ. Even after he lost the presidency to Ronald Regan in 1981, he continued his global peace efforts. As a result of this work, he was awarded a Nobel peace prize in 2002. Many of us will not achieve this level of influence or impact, but what really matters is that, 'we do whatever we can, wherever we are, whenever we can, for as long as we can with whatever we have', to try to make a difference.

Immediate impact
John, the apostle, wrote "but whoever has this world's goods, and sees his brother in need, and shuts up his heart from him, how does the love of God abide in him?"[6] When we respond to the needs of others around us we are demonstrating the abiding presence of God in us, and when we do this, we make an impact for God in the lives of those who benefit from our acts of kindness.

Many people want to meet the needs of others in practical

ways, this explains the plethora of initiatives and charities aimed at providing assistance to those in need. Through my own involvement in some initiatives of this kind, I have seen how they affect the lives of direct recipients, and society as a whole. Every time I have been able to render my assistance, I feel enriched by the experience. However I would contend that while this work is crucial, we cannot stop at this point. We need to give people an opportunity to hear of the good news of Christ and His life-changing power because doing so gives those we serve an opportunity to make a decision regarding where and how they choose to spend eternity.

Generational impact

This type of impact transcends one's lifetime; later generations will enjoy the benefits too. God introduced Himself to Moses as one who is interested in having an impact on more than one generation, in other words through generational lines. He said to Moses, "I am the God of your father - the God of Abraham, Isaac and Jacob" [7].

God wants our contribution to transcend our lifetime. Our name, integrity, enterprises, ministry and faith in Christ should be passed on to later generations. One wise man puts it this way, "the true meaning of life is to plant trees, under whose shade you do not expect to sit". People who make generational impact think long-term about how their life's work will shape things to come. They are not motivated by short-term gains or benefits.

Benjamin Disreali noted that, "the greatest good you can do for another is not just to share your riches but to reveal to him his own". When we do this, our impact transcends a life and extends to generations. It is this same principle that undergirds the idea that teaching a man to fish is a more sustainable solution to his hunger than giving him a fish to eat. By teaching him to fish, he is provided with a means to sustain himself and his family in the longer term, whereas giving him a fish maintains his dependence on others for help or assistance. It is the passing on of knowledge, understanding and the necessary resources that help to guarantee that those affected by our work also pass it on. This is what Paul hoped to achieve in his letter to Timothy,

> "You therefore, my son, be strong in the grace that is in Christ Jesus. And the things that you have heard from me among many witnesses, commit these to faithful men who will be able to teach others also." 2 Timothy 2:1-2

Eternal Impact

Reading Rick Warren's *Purpose Driven Life* several years ago drove home the point that the way I live life here on earth has eternal implications. In the book, he described life here on earth as a 'dress rehearsal' for the life that is to come. This understanding helped to shape my purpose and priorities. Eternal impact exceeds generational impact because it focuses on life beyond death and determines where we spend eternity. Jesus asked, "what shall it profit a man to gain the whole world and lose his own soul?" [8] Those who are seeking to make an eternal impact must make the souls of men their priority. The entire message of the gospel is aimed at the reconciliation of every human soul with God and every action that serves to bridge that gap is making an eternal impact.

Having been reconciled to God ourselves, as Christians we also inherit this ministry of reconciliation. Our primary mission becomes exerting godly influence here on earth and sharing the good news of the saving grace that is found only in Christ Jesus and which enables peace with God.

> "Now all things *are* of God, who has reconciled us to Himself through Jesus Christ, and has given us the ministry of reconciliation, that is, that God was in Christ reconciling the world to Himself, not imputing their trespasses to them, and has committed to us the word of reconciliation." 2 Corinthians 5: 18 - 19

Every Christian has been called and equipped to make an eternal impact in the lives of those they come in contact with. It is worth mentioning that making an eternal impact is not the reserve of pastors or those directly involved in Christian ministry. The person who invited me to the event at which I accepted Christ as my Lord and saviour, was not a pastor, but I believe that her seemingly casual invitation was noted in heaven. Every Christian has been called and equipped to make an eternal impact in the lives of those they come in contact with.

A person can make a difference, with eternal implications, in our lives even when our interaction with them has been brief or indirect, for example through reading one of their books. They might be unaware of the impact that they have made. Peter was instructed, in a God-given vision, to go to the home of a Roman centurion, Cornelius, and pray for him. At the prayer meeting that followed the Holy Spirit came upon non-Jewish believers for the first time. In this way, God rewarded the prayers and acts of devotion of Cornelius. At the same time He also expanded the understanding of the Jewish believers about the breadth of God's plan for humanity which the death and resurrection of Christ had set in motion. It seems unlikely that Peter ever saw Cornelius or the members of his household again [9]. His contact with them was fleeting, yet it had an eternal impact. Jesus was with His disciples for three years in total, yet He turned their lives around so comprehensively that they went on to live compelling lives, the effects of which are still being felt today. Eternal impact is not determined by the length of the interaction, but by the effect on people's lives.

Are you making an impact or living for an income?

Tom Brokaw, a well-known American journalist once said, "it is easy to make a buck. It is a lot tougher to make a difference". Do you agree with him? Well, I do. A person can be self-centred and become really wealthy, and yet self-centredness is incompatible with having a lasting positive effect in other people's lives. Real difference is made when we live to serve others, but you and I know that it is hard to take the focus off our own needs and concentrate instead on making a difference in the lives of others.

People who succeed at what they do are seldom motivated solely by profit, but rather their love for it and the difference they are able to make. Are you in your current job because it pays the bills and funds the lifestyle you desire, or because of the impact you are able to make? A few people have told me that their motive for working is to pay the bills and nothing more. This is very unfortunate as it means that many will remain in their jobs, trapped by the money and as a result will miss out on the chance to fulfil God's purpose for their life.

Lasting fulfilment comes from the impact we make, not the income we earn. Lasting fulfilment comes from the impact we make, not the income we earn. This might not be immediately obvious and many might, initially at least, believe that they can find fulfilment in the income they derive from a job and the lifestyle it affords them. However, I maintain that few can sustain this belief throughout their lives.

To illustrate my point let's consider a man who has successfully amassed a great deal of money- Bill Gates, the founder of Microsoft. He spent a significant part of his career building a technology empire that earned him billions of dollars, whilst making a huge difference to the lives of many people through his vision for the personal computer. By most measures, he was very successful - both financially and in terms of the contribution his products have made to humanity. However, he found he could not stop there. He has now dedicated the rest of his life to serving others by, amongst other things, working to eradicate malaria through the foundation he and his wife, Melinda, set up. I believe these two have discovered what many men and women through the ages came to realise too - making money and living solely for one's enjoyment cannot satisfy in the long run. They've chosen to make their mark on earth, and their service will not be soon forgotten.

Avoiding the trap of the 'Great Secular and Sacred Divide'

Many Christians hold the erroneous idea that some things we do are sacred, while others are secular. The notion goes something like this: you are more likely to do the kind of work that God values if you work within the church or its outreach ministries. Nothing could be further from the truth. We cannot all do church work, and I am convinced that God does not want us to either, but we can all do Christian work. By this, I mean that as Christians, we can take our values to work, no matter where or what we do.

Sometime ago, a lady told me she was considering leaving her 'secular' work to engage in full-time Christian ministry. Over the years, I have had similar conversations with a number of people, and usually, what they are really saying is that they believe that only the work that is carried out in church or parachurch organisations counts as 'Christian work'. At a recent leadership conference, Mark Greene, director of London Institute of Contemporary Christianity (LICC), described a research project involving young Christian executives in their thirties, based in Scotland. These executives worked in a wide range of vocations. The researchers discovered that despite these executives' many professional achievements, several of them could not see how their work was of value to God. As a result, while they were confident about their competency in doing their jobs, they were not confident of the 'Christian value' of their work. This highlights the disempowering effects of the 'secular-sacred divide', which suggests that some aspects of our lives matter to God more than others. Greene gave an example of a head teacher who, at the age of 34 had worked hard to turn around two failing schools and put them on the path to high achievement. Despite this she felt that she had done nothing for God. As a result of her efforts, the lives of 400 kids and their families as well the staff in both schools, were transformed. This would no doubt have had a knock-on effect on the communities in which those schools were located. Despite these achievements she did not have any sense of mission fulfilment because to her mind, her work did not directly serve God. She could not see that the effective use of her abilities in the service of others glorifies God and that everything she does, whether at work or in church matters to Him.

When Jesus commanded Christians to,

> "Let your light so shine before men that they may see your moral excellence *and* your praiseworthy, noble, *and* good deeds and recognize *and* honor *and* praise *and* glorify your Father Who is in heaven." Matthew 5: 16

He did not specify a particular geographical location or vocation. It does not matter what you are doing or where you are doing it, as long as you put all of your effort into it in order to impact lives, God is glorified through it.

CHAPTER SUMMARY
The words that we speak have great impact on others. We should use affirmative and encouraging words to help build up other's self-belief and confidence.

God wants our contribution to transcend our lifetime. Our name, integrity, enterprises, ministry and faith in Christ should be passed on to later generations.

Every Christian has been called and equipped to make an eternal impact in the lives of those they come in contact with.

Lasting fulfilment comes from the impact we make, not the income we earn. Making money and living solely for one's enjoyment cannot satisfy in the long run.

The effective use of our abilities in the service of others glorifies God and whatever we do at work or in church matters to Him. Impact is not divided between 'christian ministry' and secular life.

Make it Count

In the next ten days, make a conscious effort to focus on the seemingly insignificant things around you as you go about your daily business. Things you might ordinarily not consider to be important, such as writing a note of appreciation to your boss, or employee; have conversations on matters of faith and eternal destiny with a friend or colleague.

CHAPTER 5

BECOMING THE ONE

Being a man or a woman is a matter of birth.
Being a man or a woman who makes a difference
is a matter of choice.
- Byron Garrett

What you are is God's gift to you; what you do with
yourself is your gift to God
- Danish Proverb

Then He said to them,
'Follow Me, and I will make you fishers of men'.
- Matthew 4:19.

Everyone's life should count for something, and at some point, each person must ask themselves the question, 'what does my life count for?' In the previous chapter, I stated that God does not make junk and

Everyone's life should count for something, and at some point, each person must ask themselves the question, 'what does my life count for?

To have an impact on the lives of others, you must first understand that your life matters and that what you do makes a difference and matters to God.

every life has value before Him. While many might agree with this statement, I'm not sure that, on closer inspection, their lives bear this out.

I remember watching the 2012 London Olympics and being overcome by a feeling of ordinariness, as I watched athletes breaking records and winning medals. I found myself wondering whether, if I had taken up sport as a child I might be enjoying the kind of acclaim being garnered by the successful athletes. Aside from the fact that it is too late for me to test this hypothesis, such thoughts, if permitted to linger, would only serve to distract me from pursuing my life's mission. These 'what if...?' thoughts sidetrack us into focusing on what we can't do and hinder us from seeing what God has put within us to become.

To have an impact on the lives of others, you must first understand that your life matters and that what you do makes a difference and matters to God.

Having this threefold understanding as a basis for everything that you do, is the best foundation to build on.

In Christ, we all have capacity to do good and to be good. This capacity grows and matures as we become more aware of who we really are in relation to Him. By virtue of my work in pastoral ministry, I often visit parents of new babies and officiate naming ceremonies. On such occasions, when I look at the little bundle of joy, wrapped up and at peace with the world, a sense of hope and excitement fills my heart as I wonder what lies ahead of them. I'm eager to see their promise unfold. It is enough that they are safe and happy, and we are content with their limited capabilities at this stage, to expect anything more from a baby would be unrealistic. However, this changes as the baby grows and matures and becomes more self-aware and conscious of the world. We expect him or her to develop a sense of responsibility, which should then engender a desire to add value to the lives of those in his or her sphere of influence. This development is a continual process and it is the degree to which it is embraced that determines what we are able to offer our world. In the sections that follow I explore some of the areas of our lives in which this development should take place.

Your Identity

There is a natural human desire to define ourselves, to know who we are. This is done, first and foremost, against the backdrop of our families. We look to our relatives to tell us who we are and their lives and experiences help us to better understand our own. This is what fuels our interest in our 'roots' and has spawned an industry dedicated to helping people trace their family trees. Knowing who we are is central to our sense of belonging and the community we 'belong' to gives us a framework for deciding what constitutes appropriate behaviour. Openly identifying with, and being accepted by our families and communities is an essential part of our healthy development.

If we don't know who we are or aren't accepted by our families, we are cast adrift. The breakdown in family structures which has become prevalent in our society has had a negative effect on many people's sense of belonging. As a result, there is no place for the formation and modelling of proper decorum and behaviour.

Jesus' was part of a loving family and His earthly parents would no doubt have told Him who He was. Despite this, it was not until God affirmed Jesus as His son, that the latter was able to start His ministry or service to mankind. This public affirmation of His belonging to God's family, was an open acknowledgement of His identity and everything He did from that point onwards was inexorably linked to this identity. He was 30 years old before reaching this point, but once He got there, it took Him only three years to complete His assignment- such was the power of God's public affirmation.

> "And suddenly a voice came from heaven, saying, "This is My beloved Son, in whom I am well pleased." – Matthew 3: 17

Your real identity is not based on the name written on your birth certificate, passport or driver's license. It is much deeper, it's the essence of your being. Identity is about our sense of self in relation to our source - God.

Identity is about our sense of self in relation to our source - God.

In the same way that we grow in our awareness of being a member of our various families, when we become Christians we grow in our awareness of belonging to God's family. In this family we are co-heirs with Christ in God's kingdom.

> "This resurrection life you [Christians] received from God is not a timid, grave-tending life. It's adventurously expectant, greeting God with a

childlike 'what's next, Papa?' God's Spirit touches
our spirit and confirms who we really are. We
know who He is, and we know who we are: Father
and children. And we know we are going to get
what's coming to us—an unbelievable inheritance!
We go through exactly what Christ goes through.
If we go through the hard times with him, then
we're certainly going to go through the good times
with him!" - Romans 8: 15 - 17 (Message)

The word 'identity' is derived from a Latin word - identitās,
which means 'the same'. The image that comes to mind
when I think of the word i*dentity* is a long cylindrical stick
of sweet known colloquially as 'rock'. This sweet is often
sold at seaside destinations around the UK and usually has
the name of the locality in which it is sold, embossed
through its core, for example 'Brighton Rock'. No matter
what point you break the sweet, the name can be seen on
the exposed core. In other words, any part of the sweet
could be traced to its source. This is analogous to our
identity.

When God told the children of Israel

"Listen to Me, you who follow after righteousness,
You who seek the LORD: Look to the rock *from
which* you were hewn, And to the hole of the pit

from which you were dug. Look to Abraham your father, And to Sarah *who* bore you; For I called him alone, And blessed him and increased him." - Isaiah 51: 1 - 2

He was trying to evoke their sense of identity, which has its root in Abraham, their forefather. As a Christian, my identity is grounded in who I have become in Christ. As I grow in this understanding, I am increasingly aware that my work here on earth should mirror that of Jesus over two millennia ago- loving God and loving people. Doing so becomes a daily exercise in self-actualization, and each day presents me with the opportunity to show forth more of who I really am in Christ.

Our Values

Our values flow from our sense of identity. During my childhood years, my dad would gently caution my siblings and I against forgetting whose children we were. Obviously, he didn't mean this literally. What he was trying to do was to help us see a link between our identity, as members of the Akinlade family, and the values we lived by. In the same way, when our identity is established in God, the values that shape our lives must be determined by His, as set out in the bible.

Because values are so strongly tied to our identity, they are central to our lives. They are the 'bottom line' and they determine the things we prioritise in our lives. The scriptures give us an indication of what our two main priorities should be- loving God and loving other people.

Overall, the bible is a sound basis for shaping the values of Christians even in our post-modern world. The values Jesus upheld such as love, truth and service should still constitute the core values of every Christian. If, as is commonly suggested, we are the product of all the choices and decisions we make, then we are ultimately shaped by our core values, as these determine our choices and decisions.

Every individual functions according to a system of values. Every individual functions according to a system of values. These values can be good or bad and may be consciously or unconsciously formed. In other words, we can consider and then choose the values we want to live by or we can passively absorb those of our society or family and friends. However we arrive at them, they serve us best when we are clear what our values are before we face challenging circumstances. This increases the chance that we'll act appropriately when confronted with difficult choices. Serving others is a great value to have, but you're more likely to actually live by it, if you have clearly articulated and committed to it before you are called to serve in a capacity that will disrupt your preferred way of life.

Our Gifting

When each of us was created, God placed within us certain gifts, in order that we might serve others. We were not consulted, and we are unaware of our gifts at birth. However, as we grow and learn more about ourselves, our distinctive gifts become evident to us and to others.

In the parable of the talents, the master gave "talents" of varying amounts to his servants for investment purposes. It is to this same end that God gives us gifts - to add value. We need to see our gifts as akin to the "talents" in the parable, which God has given us to use in serving others. Like the third servant, many of us have buried our gifts because they seem insignificant or we are risk-averse. We just don't see them as gifts. That's why it's important that we identify and value our gifts appropriately and that we develop the confidence to use them

On the other hand, acknowledging our gifts and their source should keep us humble because we recognise that we are simply recipients, we haven't earned them. Gifts are allocated so that each person can play a distinct role as part of the greater whole.

For I say, through the grace given to me, to everyone who is among you, not to think of himself more highly than he ought to think, but to think soberly, as God has dealt to each one a measure of faith. For as we have many members in one body, but all the members do not have the same function, so we, being many, are one body in Christ, and individually members of one another. Having then gifts differing according to the grace that is given to us, let us use them: if prophecy, let us prophesy in proportion to our faith; or ministry, let us use it in our ministering; he who teaches, in teaching; he who exhorts, in exhortation; he who gives, with liberality; he who leads, with diligence; he who shows mercy, with cheerfulness. Romans 12:3-8

So if you're persuaded that everyone has a gift, the next pertinent question is: 'how do you spot yours?' Examining the things that you do with minimal effort, compared to other people, is a good place to start. Determining gifts and strengths is a popular endeavour and as a result many assessment tools have been developed to help people in their search. These tools adopt a range of approaches, from the spiritual through to the psychological. While I have found some of these tools useful, I think they serve us best when we ask God for wisdom with regards to how best to use them.

Over the course of my adult life, I have used a number of these 'gift identification' assessments and the results have been pretty consistent. For example, one of the gifts that these tests consistently identify is my ability to identify gifts in others. Until recently, I did not appreciate this ability as a God-given gift, until I began to notice how easily I am able to allocate resources to areas where they can be best utilised. This gift enables me, to a large degree, to do my job which involves deploying and managing a large volunteer workforce. It was also a factor in my decision to set up *Enability*, a social enterprise which helps ex-offenders become gainfully employed.

An unidentified and unused gift remains mere potential. Myles Monroe, the 'leadership and purpose' guru, is often quoted as saying,

An unidentified and unused gift remains mere potential.

> "the wealthiest places in the world are not the gold mines of South America or the oil fields of Iraq or Iran. They're not the diamond mines of South Africa or the banks of the world. The wealthiest place on the planet is just down the road. It is the cemetery. There lie buried, companies that were never started, inventions that were never made, bestselling books that were never written and

masterpieces that were never painted. In the cemetery is buried the greatest treasure of untapped potential".

There's truth in his observation. It's also true that the world will be worse off if you do not identify and utilise your gifts. Gifts have to be discovered and developed, before they can be deployed effectively.

Skill

Skill differs from gifts in that the former is given while the latter is acquired. A gift must be honed, through much practice and acquired knowledge in order for it to become a skill. You and I are not responsible for the gifts we have, but turning them into skills is very much our responsibility.

I'm saddened when people's gifts remain dormant. Unfortunately, this isn't a rare occurrence; it takes effort and commitment to develop skill and not everyone is willing to put in the work required. Your gift might get you noticed, but it is unlikely to keep you noticed.

A man's gift makes room for him, And brings him before great men- Proverbs 18: 16.

In this day and age, we need Christians who have honed their gifts into skills so that they're equipped to best serve society by working towards the good of its members.

In the bible, we read the story of Joseph - a young man with a gift for visionary dreams and dream interpretation. Unfortunately, in the beginning, he lacked the skill of tact when sharing these dreams and their interpretation. As a result of this deficiency he was sold into slavery by his brothers, who were deeply offended by his tactless approach to sharing his dreams. Over the years, having suffered great hardships he developed the skills of tact and visionary wisdom, and he was able to use his gift for the benefit of others. As a result, he was elevated from his miserable state in an Egyptian prison to the position of Prime Minister and given access to the palace of Pharaoh. He'd obviously learnt a lot from his experiences as there was a vast difference between the way he had relayed his dreams to his father and siblings years earlier, and the way he delivered the interpretation of the dreams of the butler and the baker and later, Pharaoh. His gift for interpreting dreams brought him before Pharaoh, but it was his tact, wisdom and visionary leadership that made him an effective Prime Minister in Pharaoh's Egypt.

To live a life that counts, we cannot afford to function merely at the level of our gifts, we must work to develop them so that we become very proficient in deploying them. Henry David Thoreau once said 'Not only must we be good, but we must also be good for something'. I recently had a conversation with a young lady in which she excitedly told me that she had discovered her area of gifting and was certain that God had called her to work with children. I shared her excitement but gently pointed out that identifying a calling to work with children was just the first step. In order to become a person of influence in the area God had called her to, she would have to do the work of identifying the age-group she wanted to work with and then develop the skills to serve them.

It is our skills and not our undeveloped gifts, that are of most value to others. Employers don't hire on the basis of gifts or the promise of potential, nor do they award promotions on those bases. Similarly, you're unlikely to attract investment or clients for your business based on your gifts. Investors and clients are interested in who you are, but they care just as much, if not more, about what you can *do*.

Vision

The word 'vision' essentially means to see what's in front of us or things that are to come. Vision, in this context has nothing to do with the physical eye, rather it relates to the ability of the mind to paint a picture of a preferable future. A compelling vision has the power to define the course of one's life, and by extension, impact the lives of many others.

We become and achieve what we see. The pertinent question then is, 'what do you see?' There are people whose **We become and achieve what we see.** vision is only large enough for themselves but there are some who see beyond themselves. In life, generally, those who only 'see' for themselves make an insignificant impact, but those whose vision is large enough to accommodate others end up effecting far-reaching change. That's what happens when you take the focus off yourself and instead concentrate on serving and building up others.

William Carey, the great English missionary to India had a vision of the nation of India becoming aware of Jesus. At that time, in England there **Carey expected great things of God, and so he attempted great things for God.** wasn't a missionary society or a widespread interest in missions. Against this background of extreme apathy, Carey persevered and saw his vision fulfilled. By the time of his death in 1834, at the age of 73, he had seen the bible translated into forty different languages. He'd worked as a college professor, and founded a college. He had seen India open its doors to missionaries, the passing of an edict prohibiting *sati* (the burning of widows on the funeral pyres of their dead husbands), and he had seen many converts to Christianity [1]. Carey expected great things of God, and so he attempted great things for God.

The world we live in today is a product of the visions and dreams of those who came before us. The famous Martin Luther King's 'I Have a Dream speech greatly influenced the course of racial equality in America. Almost 40 years since he publicly articulated his vision, it is becoming a reality in America's multiracial society. The United States currently has an African-American President, an unimaginable possibility in the days of Martin Luther King Jnr. Though he is long gone, his vision is coming to pass.

Visions don't have to be grand or ground-breaking. What makes for a worthwhile vision is its ability to advance the well-being of others. Most of us will not have visions of changing the world, but we can begin to see what we do in the light of the impact it can have on the lives of those around us. I am more impressed by people who aspire to see their own little corner of the world changed, than by those who have visions of changing the world but do nothing to improve the lives of those around them. God gave Abraham a vision for the birth of a whole nation, but he wasn't so consumed by this lofty calling as to be unconcerned about the well-being of Lot, his cousin, or the people of Sodom. This demonstrates that he was not just a blessed man, he chose to be a blessing too.

Blessed but Broken

Two separate bible accounts describe Jesus feeding thousands of people from small quantities of food. The book of Matthew records both occasions. On the first occasion [2], He was handed a little boy's lunch of five loaves and two fish, which He took, blessed and broke before handing it back to the disciples to distribute to the multitude who were huddled in groups. On the second occasion [3], things followed a similar pattern. Jesus blessed the loaves and again broke them, and instructed that they should be shared amongst the people.

Many Christians will recognise this pattern of breaking and multiplication in their own lives. However, many of us may struggle to reconcile our blessedness with our brokenness and we wonder why, if indeed we are blessed, we go through seasons of painful stretching. How can we be blessed, yet suffer prolonged barrenness, or be blessed and broke or unemployed, or suffer from ill health?

What strikes me as I read the stories of Jesus feeding the multitude is that the loaves served more people when they were broken. Many times, when we go through these phases, we automatically conclude that it is not possible to be blessed *and* be experiencing such brokenness. This way of thinking often causes us to lose sight of what God wants to do through our brokenness. Not every Christian will experience prolonged seasons of hardship but those that do, need not doubt their blessedness. Instead we ought to develop the understanding that often, these seasons pave the way for God to use our lives for His glory.

Both stories of multiplication end with a mention of surplus food being collected after all the people had eaten and were satisfied. The bible does not tell us what was done with the surplus but I imagine the little child being given a take-away pack in acknowledgment of his sacrifice in sharing his lunch.

Regardless of our state in life, we can count for something. We are blessed and that is settled. This understanding enables us to work our way into being a blessing. Many years ago, when it seemed as if nothing was working for me, I often swung between hope and despair but whenever I managed to remember my state of blessedness, even in the toughest times, I was able to be a blessing to others. During that period, I only experienced peace when I allowed the Christ-infused life that was within me to flow out to others.

CHAPTER SUMMARY

As humans, we need to know who we are. Our sense of identity defines us and helps to shape the person we become.

Seeing ourselves as part of God's family will cause us to act in ways consistent to God's nature and personality. Jesus had a strong sense of His identity in God, because God affirmed Him.

Every human being is created with unique gifts from God and it is our responsibility to discover, develop and deploy them.

Visions don't have to be grand or ground-breaking. What makes for a worthwhile vision is its ability to advance the wellbeing of others.

We sometimes go through brokenness before we can become a blessing.

Make it Count

It is through our daily actions and decisions that we are able to make long-lasting contributions to the lives of others. Identity is the basis of our values. Consider some new habits that you need to cultivate in order to live by values that are consistent with your membership of God's family. For example, serving others is a worthwhile value, so deciding to seek out opportunities that enable you to serve others on a daily basis is a good habit to cultivate.

CHAPTER 6

THE SACRIFICE OF ONE

The first question which the priest and the Levite asked was: "If I stop to help this man, what will happen to me?" But... the good Samaritan reversed the question: "If I do not stop to help this man, what will happen to him?"
- Martin Luther King, Jnr

If you pursue good with labor, the labor passes away but the good remains
- Cicero

Most assuredly, I say to you, unless a grain of wheat falls into the ground and dies, it remains alone; but if it dies, it produces much grain.
- John 12: 24

Recently, I saw an episode of the popular television series, 24. In this episode, Gael Ortega, played by Jesse Borrego, placed himself at risk of exposure to a deadly biological virus, whilst trying to prevent an explosion that would disperse it. His aim was to stop the bomb from being detonated, causing the virus to spread over a large area and as a consequence killing many innocent people. It was a risky and ultimately futile effort. He became the first casualty of the deadly virus and eventually died.

Many action movies incorporate similar all-or-nothing, do-or-die scenes of brave, selfless sacrifice, and this is what many of us have come to associate with true sacrifice. I have learnt that sacrifice doesn't have to be at that level to be heroic. Adopting a child, running an after-school club for kids in deprived communities, feeding the hungry in your community, or even giving of your financial substance to worthy causes are examples of small but important sacrifices that people make on a daily basis.

To live a life that counts is to commit to sacrificing one's time, money and energy. There is a cost to a life of significance. God sacrificed His only son. He paid a high price for the salvation of the whole world. In a bid to redeem His creation, God implemented a costly plan. He gave up His only son, who knew no sin, [1] to bear our guilt so that all humanity would have the opportunity to be reconciled with

Him and regain our place of dominion.

> [The Lamb of God] The next day John saw Jesus coming toward him, and said, "Behold! The Lamb of God who takes away the sin of the world!
> - John 1: 29

> All who dwell on the earth will worship him, whose names have not been written in the Book of Life of the Lamb slain from the foundation of the world. Revelations 13: 8

Sacrifice involves giving up something precious for the sake of something else that is considered to have higher value or significance. Therefore, you're not making a sacrifice if what you're giving up is not important to you. Every commitment demands a sacrifice, and real change only happens where there has been a sacrifice of some sort.

Every commitment demands a sacrifice, and real change only happens where there has been a sacrifice of some sort.

Time

In our busy world, time is precious and we can often find it difficult to sacrifice. Technology and (mostly) growing disposable incomes have helped us save some time with fast-food drive-throughs, online banking, automatic car wash, microwaves etc. but for the most part this 'saved' time has simply been diverted to the many leisure activities that now preoccupy us.

Some of us manage to eke out a little time to share with our friends and loved ones, but how about giving our time to those that God knows – all people? True, we may not be able to help everybody, but helping the stranger or the outsider is something that God cares about, and so, it should also be our priority.

Jesus sacrificed a lot more than we may think. For the most part, when we think of Jesus' time on earth we only consider the fact that He gave His physical life for all humanity. But as the son of God, He gave up eternity and stepped into our time-bound reality with all its attending limitations.

In the parable of the Good Samaritan [2], Jesus never tells us why the priest and the Levite didn't stop to help the injured man, but I speculate that the priest and the Levite were probably in a hurry to get to their destinations. Perhaps, they were already running late for some important religious appointment. I think if we're honest many of us are closer to the priest and the Levite, than we'd like to be. There's only one remedy- slow down! Only by slowing down, or even stopping, are we able to observe the plights of those around us and respond appropriately. In teaching a lesson on loving one's neighbour, Jesus was also trying to align our priorities. I believe He deliberately left out the details of the three travellers' destinations. I think that He wanted us to understand that compared to the plight of the wounded man, the travellers' destinations and appointments were unimportant.

The Samaritan was not on an aimless stroll when he was confronted with the beaten, half-dead man. The Samaritan had a set destination in mind, but when he saw the man lying on the ground, he took pity on him and allowed his own plans to be interrupted. I don't imagine for a minute that this choice was convenient, but he had his priorities right; he knew what was truly important.

A few years ago, after reading this very parable, I had an opportunity to practice what I had learnt, but I failed to take it. I was walking from Kings College University, where I was a student, towards the underground station. I was on my way home. As I approached the station, I saw a man lying by the roadside. He was lying so still, I wondered if he might be dead. I looked around and noticed that others were just passing by, no one stopped to attend to the man. I stood there for a couple of minutes contemplating what to do, and then I joined the others who were walking by. I left the man there and went on my way to fulfill my other 'priorities'. I felt really bad afterwards and have since repented, but I still wonder what happened to that man.

The truth is that our time is not really ours to spend as we like. Managing our time well remains an all-important issue. The truth is that our time is not really ours to spend as we like. It belongs to God and He has given us stewardship over it. Suffice to say, He alone should determine how we use it. Jesus set out the top two priorities for every Christian's life and these should guide how we spend our time. We are to (1) Love God with all of our hearts and (2) Love our neighbours as we love ourselves [3]. When we give of our time, sacrificially, to others as unto God, we are simply acknowledging His Lordship over our lives. After all, if we're unable to serve the neighbour that we do see, what is the likelihood that we'll be able to serve a God whom we do not?

Treasures

I find the biblical parable about the "rich fool" [4], very intriguing. For one thing, the prospect of a rich, but foolish person contradicts much of the popular narrative about wealthy people in our modern world. Today, although I suspect it has always been this way, we often associate wealth with intelligence. At the very least we expect a rich person to be able to pay for wise counsel so that he or she can make good decisions and at least appear wise. Yet in this story, the rich man was considered a fool. Why? Jesus points to the rich man's plans to spend his wealth as evidence of his foolishness. Though the man had enjoyed a bumper harvest that year, his only thoughts were about how he might hoard his great harvest and what personal merriment his wealth would afford him, rather than how it might enable him to be a blessing to others.

> And I will say to my soul, "Soul, you have many goods laid up for many years; take your ease; eat, drink, *and* be merry."' But God said to him, 'Fool! This night your soul will be required of you; then whose will those things be which you have provided?' – Luke 12: 19 - 20

We learn here that what is most important is not really what we have, but how we use what we have. We also learn that none of the things we accumulate during our time on earth will be of value to us when we die. It will all be left behind for others when **what is most important is not really what we have, but how we use what we have.** we are gone. Holding on too tightly to our earthly treasures is foolishness because every passing moment draws us closer to our death and so pulls us away from our treasures on earth.

This is why Jesus said we should concentrate our efforts on those things that will have a lasting significance rather than those things that lose value

> Do not lay up for yourselves treasures on earth, where moth and rust destroy and where thieves break in and steal; but lay up for yourselves treasures in heaven, where neither moth nor rust destroys and where thieves do not break in and steal. – Matthew 6: 19 - 20

The dictionary defines 'treasure' as "wealth and riches, usually hoarded, especially in the form of money, precious metals, or gems".

God's treasures are in people Jesus has shown us that the best place to invest is in a 'heavenly bank account'. How do we do this? We know we can't courier our treasure to heaven and we also know that when we die, we cannot take our accumulated wealth with us, so how then do we make deposits into this account? According to the bible, it's by investing our wealth in people. More specifically by using our wealth to alleviate the suffering of those less privileged than us, and by propagating the good news about Jesus and the kingdom of God to as many people as possible. God's treasures are in people; "But we have this treasure in earthen vessels, that the excellence of the power may be of God and not of us" – 2 Corinthians 4: 7 and He expects us to do likewise.

I once heard Rick Warren echo a quote originally attributed to Winston Churchill, he said, "We make a living by what we get, but make a life by what we give. No one is remembered by what they earned, it is by what they gave". Those words have stuck with me ever since.

In chapter ten of the book of Mark, we read of the rich young ruler who asked Jesus what it would take to inherit eternal life. Jesus advised him to follow the law. The young man informed Jesus he was already a strict adherent of the law. Those who overheard the exchange might have been impressed by the rich young ruler's personal discipline, but Jesus, knowing that something was missing, asked him to do something that would reveal his true priorities. Jesus asked him to sacrifice all that he had, by giving it to the poor. Unfortunately, that was too great a price for the rich young ruler to pay, so he walked away from the offer of eternal life. The issue here, was not so much his wealth, but where his focus lay. He'd chosen to focus on things with no eternal significance.

When I first read this story, I wondered why Jesus didn't press the point about eternal life with the rich ruler. After all, that was why Jesus came to earth- to provide all mankind with access to eternal life. However, with time I realised what Jesus instinctively recognised; the young ruler was not unaware of what was at stake. His unwillingness to sacrifice it in order to gain eternal life was a clear response to Jesus' offer [5]. As in other character-revealing stories described in scripture, the rich ruler, by his own choices, had determined his own destiny. When we sacrifice our wealth by giving it away to improve the conditions of others, we are indicating what is important to us. What we are really saying is that our wealth is mainly a God-given tool to be used to enrich the lives of others, and is not an end in itself.

Talents

Much has already been written in this book about our talents and our judicious use of them as we seek to live lives that count. I hope that I've successfully made the case for treating the use of our God-given talents as a responsibility that must be faithfully discharged. By this I mean that God gives us unique talents so that we can use them to serve other people.

Successful and fulfilled people are those who manage to utilise their talents daily. It is easy to conclude that if you are doing work that is in alignment with your gifts, you should love doing it and everyday should be a walk in the proverbial park. This simply isn't so. In fact there will be many times when it is hard, unrewarding and even tedious.

When you're aware of your gift and are actively seeking to develop it, the early days are often the 'honeymoon phase' because of the excitement and passion you feel whenever you use your gift. So much so that you're eager to volunteer your services at any given opportunity. However it's often the case that as you develop your gift and there's more demand for your skills, this eagerness wanes, especially when your efforts are not fully appreciated.

So, what you were once willing to give freely, you now need an acute sense of responsibility and commitment to continue to provide. This is the point at which the serving others with your gifts becomes a sacrifice. In other words, it is your recognition of the gift of God in your life and the purpose for which it was given- to benefit others- which drives you to continue to share your gift.

The film, Chariots of Fire tells the story of scotsman Eric Liddel, a British Olympian and missionary who as a gifted athlete recognised his talent and used it for God's purpose. He said,

'I believe God made me for a purpose, but he also made me fast. And when I run I feel His pleasure.

Liddel used his athletic talents to glorify God, and indeed God was glorified through his life. When we are using our talents for God's purpose, we bring Him Glory and that's when we feel His pleasure the most.

no man achieves any significant feat for God without paying a price. Competing as a world-class athlete requires significant physical exertion and self-denial. As a gold medallist in the 400m race at the 1924 Paris Olympics, Liddel understood the sacrifice required to fully develop one's talents for God's glory. He understood that no man achieves any significant feat for God without paying a price.

On a number of occasions, William Wilberforce the politician and great abolitionist thought of giving up the fight against the slave trade because of the enormous opposition and discouragement he faced. In a letter, believed to be John Wesley's last, he encouraged Wilberforce to persevere in his fight to abolish the British slave trade. Wesley wrote,

"unless God has raised you up for this very thing [of fighting the "execrable villainy" of the slave trade], you will be worn out by the opposition of men and devils. But if God be for you, who can be against you? Are all of them together stronger than God? O be not weary of well doing!"

Though God had blessed Wilberforce with many talents including the oratorical ability, which equipped him for the role he was to play in the abolishment of the slave trade, the victory only came through enormous sacrifice.

Jesus demonstrated, through the example of His own life, the importance of sacrifice. He gave to and served His disciples and followers willingly. The sacrifice of His life, on the cross, made it possible for the whole of humanity to be reconciled to God. Jesus used the seed analogy to explain the sacrificial life. He said "Very truly I tell you, unless a kernel of wheat falls to the ground and dies, it remains only a single seed. But if it dies, it produces many seeds"[6]. For the kernel of wheat to live beyond itself, it has to die. In this context, death is a metaphor for sacrifice, and like the kernel of wheat, when we sacrifice, the yield is greater than the cost to us.

CHAPTER SUMMARY

To live a life that counts is to commit to sacrificing one's time, money and energy to the service of others. There is a cost to a life of significance.

Jesus demonstrated, through the example of His own life, the importance of sacrifice. He gave to and served His disciples and followers willingly.

Helping the vulnerable in our society, such as the stranger or the socially excluded is something God particularly cares about.

When we give our time to others, we are simply acknowledging Jesus' lordship over our lives. Our service to the neighbour that we do see, is a good indicator of our love towards a God that we can't see.

Holding on too tightly to our earthly treasures is foolishness because every passing moment draws us closer to our death and so pulls us away from our treasures on earth.

Make it Count

There is no *prize* without a *price*. Write down the some of the things you'd like to achieve in life, now write down the price you are willing to pay for them.

I press toward the goal for the prize of the upward call of God in Christ Jesus. - Philippians 3: 14

CHAPTER 7

THE CHALLENGE OF ONE

Security is mostly a superstition. It does not exist in nature, nor do the children of men as a whole experience it. Avoiding danger is no safer in the long run than outright exposure. Life is either a daring adventure or nothing. – Helen Keller

Where there is progress there is bound to be opposition

I have been constantly on the move. I have been in danger from rivers, in danger from bandits, in danger from my fellow Jews, in danger from Gentiles; in danger in the city, in danger in the country, in danger at sea; and in danger from false believers
- 2 Corinthians 11: 24 - 28 (NIV)

The number and intensity of the challenges we face are often commensurate with the extent to which our actions will disrupt the status quo . Not every challenge is a direct consequence of the positive impact we're making, but every positive impact will trigger a commensurate challenge. Physics teaches us that there is a degree of resistance (friction) when two parts rub against one another. So if you're doing anything worthwhile you should expect to have to deal with some opposition, this might come from others or even, from within yourself.

Jesus faced both types of challenge. Firstly, the bible records many occasions in which his own community resisted Him. John 1: 11 records, 'He [Jesus] came to His own, and His own did not receive Him'. They opposed Him, they opposed His message, His method of ministry and His mission. They expected a deliverer from God but their preconceived notions and their stubborn certainty about their own ways of doing things meant they were unable to recognise the fulfilment of their expectations (Jesus) when it came.

Jesus also faced challenges within. As the time drew near for Him to embark on the final leg of His mission, His human frailty came to the fore and He became very distressed at the thought of a painful death and the weight of sin that He would have to bear. He was fully aware that bearing the sin of the entire human race would mean a time of separation from God; something He had never had to face before. In the face of this crushing prospect, He nearly buckled under the pressure. It took prayer and the assistance of God's angels to strengthen His resolve. He had the option of backing out, but thank God, He chose to follow through for the sake of humanity.

> "Then an angel appeared to Him from heaven, strengthening Him. And being in agony, He prayed more earnestly. Then His sweat became like great drops of blood falling down to the ground"
> – Luke 22: 43 - 44

Apostle Paul also faced both internal and external challenges. In one of his letters to the early Corinthian church, he wrote, "For indeed, when we came to Macedonia, our bodies had no rest, but we were troubled on every side. *Outside* were conflicts, *inside* were fears"[1]. In spite of these conflicts and fears, he found the courage and strength to carry on.

Is God trying to tell me something?

A common reaction to challenges is doubt about the merits of one's actions or course. People often wonder whether God is trying to tell them, through the challenges they're facing, to stop doing whatever it is they're doing. Well, perhaps. But then again, maybe not. Challenges are not

Challenges are not necessarily an indication that you're outside of the will of God. In fact, you could be right in the centre of God's will. necessarily an indication that you're outside of the will of God. In fact, you could be right in the centre of God's will. The challenges you're facing could simply be a direct (and expected) opposition by the devil, to the work you're involved in. There have been instances in my life when I doubted that I was doing right by God, because of the challenges I faced. In those times, the guidance I received from God's Word just seemed misguided in the light of the challenges. Where I initially rested on the certainty of God's Word, I became confused and unsure. I think many Christians will relate to the scenario I have described. I found it helpful to remember that Jesus had to deal with challenges in His bid to bring salvation to humanity, so did Apostle Paul while trying to spread the gospel and yet, both of them were doing what God had commanded.

It may be true that challenges are God's megaphone to rouse us [2], however I am persuaded that God will not put us through perpetual pain in order to teach us a lesson. I believe if God is trying to tell us something through a challenge it will become clear that God is at work. This is why it's so important to pray and ask God about the challenges we face. By doing this, we are more than likely to get clarity about the nature of the challenges we are facing from His word or through the insight and wisdom of other faithful believers.

Why do we face challenges?

The nature and intensity of the challenges we face vary but they are not uncommon to man. In other words, there is nothing you are going through or are likely to go through that someone, somewhere hasn't experienced before. In addition, they serve similar purposes in our lives.

> "No trial has overtaken you that is not faced by others. And God is faithful: He will not let you be tried beyond what you are able to bear, but with the trial will also provide a way out so that you may be able to endure it." - 1 Corinthians 10: 13

While it is important not to focus excessively on challenges, it is also important to understand their source and the purpose they serve in our lives. The devil plots and schemes in order to frustrate our attempts at making positive changes in the world, by setting up challenges against us. His mission daily is to work hard at ensuring that we do not make it through the day victorious. That doesn't mean that the effects of all challenges are evil. God allows certain challenges to come our way, not to frustrate us but to set us up for greater and better things. The story of Joseph is a case in point. He faced all sorts of challenges at the hands of his brothers, Potiphar's wife, and whilst in prison, but all these were tools in God's hands. They prepared him and ultimately got him to his destined place as second-in-command to Pharaoh. Addressing the brothers who sold him into slavery, he said:

> "But now, do not therefore be grieved or angry with yourselves because you sold me here; for God sent me before you to preserve life."
> - Genesis 45: 5

The book of Daniel, in the bible, tells the story of three Hebrew boys, namely Shadrach, Meshach, and Abed-Nego. These three boys were exiles in Babylon after the defeat of their nation by the Babylonian king, Nebuchadnezzar. They were confronted with a life-threatening choice: to bow down and worship the king's golden image, and in so doing dishonour God, or accept the excruciatingly painful experience of being burnt alive. It was a test of their resolve to follow God and I consider their example amongst the most inspiring in the bible.

> "They said, 'O Nebuchadnezzar, we have no need to answer you in this matter. If that *is the case,* our God whom we serve is able to deliver us from the

burning fiery furnace, and He will deliver *us* from your hand, O king. But if not, let it be known to you, O king, that we do not serve your gods, nor will we worship the gold image which you have set up'" – Daniel 3: 16 – 18

There are lessons to be learnt from the way Shadrach, Meshach, and Abed-Nego responded to the challenge they faced.

Firstly, in the face of the challenge, they were persuaded that God was able to deliver them (vs. 17). Such faith does not suddenly appear in the heat of a challenge. It is established long before one is faced with any questions about God's ability. When you think of the wonders of creation, the cycles of life and all the other things God made, it is not hard to acknowledge that God's ability is boundless. In my experience the problem for many people, both Christians and non-Christians, isn't with the idea that God is able to deliver. Their doubts tend to centre on whether He will deliver *for them*.

It is the idea of God's willingness to come through for us in the midst of our challenges that many people grapple with. I know people who believe in God's ability, and even have no qualms believing that God will come through for their friend or someone else. They even pray for others and see results, but they struggle to believe the same for themselves in the midst of their own challenges.

Challenges reveal the true state of our faith in a way that few other things can. The three Hebrew boys didn't doubt God's ability to save them. Their confidence in God transcended their situation. This is why they were able to say, "But if not, let it be known to you, O king, that we do not serve your gods, nor will we worship the gold image which you have set up'". In that moment they acknowledged the sovereignty of God. It is that margin that allows God to be God in our lives. When facing challenges, a pertinent question to consider is, 'what if God does not deliver me from this challenge?' To be honest, this is not something I like to contemplate and I am sure you don't either, but the reality of the matter is that there are times that things do not go the way we want them to. I am not trying to rationalise doubt here, I'm trying to get you to honestly consider the state of your faith by considering the question, 'if things do not go the way I want, is God still God and, *my* God at that? Challenges reveal the true state of our faith in a way that few other things can.

In the case of these three Hebrew boys, they were thrown into the fiery furnace for their defiant faith but a fourth man appeared in the fire with them. They were delivered, and were promoted by the very king who had been the instrument of their gruelling test of faith. Above all, God got the glory because a decree was made by the king that "any people, nation, or language which speaks anything amiss against the God of Shadrach, Meshach, and Abed-Nego shall be cut in pieces, and their houses shall be made an ash heap; because there is no other God who can deliver like this."[3]

Don't Quit

Contrary to the popular saying, death and taxes are not the only things that are inevitable in life. Ahead of any major breakthrough, challenges are also inevitable. Unfortunately, many of us give up too soon, so we don't get to see the new era of our lives that lie on the other side of the challenge. I think if most of us, only knew how close we were to the edge of significance, we would push on and refuse to be overcome by our challenges. As the saying goes, quitters never overcome and overcomers never quit.

There are many challenges that we might face on our journey to significance that could cause us to consider quitting. In his book, *When You See the Invisible, You Can Do the Impossible*, Oral Roberts wrote of the financial challenges he faced at a time during the early days of his ministry that almost caused him to quit. At the time, the challenges made him angry and shook his faith terribly, so

Everyone who lives a significant life must be well past the point where quitting is a serious option. much so that he spoke and acted in ways that, on reflection, he is not proud of. According to him, incidents like this and others taught him that things are not always going to be easy, and that often times, one may even feel like quitting. Oral Roberts is not the only one who has ever felt like quitting, even Jesus felt this way, but He stayed the course. Everyone who lives a significant life must be well past the point where quitting is a serious option. They may seriously consider it but they manage to get beyond it. Recently, at a church volunteers workshop I was invited to speak at in northern England, one of the delegates asked how one finds the strength and will to continue to serve as a leader even in the face of challenges. I explained that many leaders are, at some point, tempted to quit. The thing that keeps them going beyond this 'quitting' point is the strength of their connectedness to their core values. This is why being clear about what your values are *before* you face a challenge is so important. For me, on the occasions when I have considered quitting, what has kept me going is the thought of the negative impact my decision to quit will have on the people I serve and by extension, the kingdom of God.

Thank God Oral Roberts did not quit. Following that incident, referred to above in November 1947, he picked himself up, continued to trust God, and went on to trust Him with even bigger faith projects. In 1963, Roberts founded the Oral Roberts University, which is now the most notable Charismatic Christian University in the world.[4]

Dealing with Challenges

The bible doesn't prescribe a 'one size fits all' approach to dealing with challenges. A look through scriptures shows that God brings about deliverance in many different ways and so it would be unwise to outline any approach as the sure-fire way to overcome challenges. More than any strategy, what's important is to have the assurance that God is in the situation with you. In the heat of a challenge God's presence isn't always obvious or foremost in our minds, We might ask, like Gideon whose nation was struggling under the oppression of the neighbouring Midianites, "but 'if the LORD is with us, why then has all this happened?" [5]. In other words why would an all-powerful God allow us to face enormous challenges when He is able to prevent them? It's tempting to conclude therefore that God is no longer present with us, or perhaps wasn't with us in the first place. However, nothing can be further from the truth as revealed in the bible. The bible is full of examples of, and promises about, His abiding presence. One of my favourite scriptures states "...For He Himself has said, 'I will never leave you nor forsake you'"[6]. In this scripture Jesus' promise to be ever-present, no matter what I am going through, comes through loud and clear.

Having an assurance of His presence is the starting point for dealing with any challenge. I once heard a preacher say that "when you see the magnitude of God, then every challenge becomes manageable", and I agree with this. David had the same understanding when he faced Goliath[7]. So, to overcome challenges, you must first clearly identify the challenger then, you must realise that the battle is the Lord's [8]. As a man accustomed to battles, David always got God involved in every battle he fought and he did this by asking God for a battle strategy, each time he was to go into battle. While most of us will not face physical combat, David's strategy of asking for divine assistance still applies. Except in our case, Christ has gone before us and has claimed victory on our behalf, and we are simply enforcing and securing what has already been won. We do this by praying and meditating on the word of God until we are fully persuaded of the reality of God's promise.

Everyone goes through challenges; I certainly have, and while I don't relish the prospect, I expect to face challenges in future. Several years ago, I observed a dear friend go through a prolonged period (five years) of unemployment. Up to that point, he had enjoyed a very successful career.

He was an intelligent and hardworking fellow, and the organisation he worked for at the time rewarded him with a large salary and very attractive bonuses.

His troubles started when the IT bubble burst. Unfortunately, the company he worked for was one of the early casualties of the disintegration of the IT boom. When the company's operation shrank, many staff, including my friend, were made redundant. He wasn't overly alarmed. He was fairly confident that the redundancy pay-off would tide him over till he found another job. Given his track-record it was reasonable to assume that he would find another job quite quickly. The first few months came and went. Then the months rolled into a year and then into two and so on, without any job in sight. All this while, he kept praying and believing that God would help him find another job in the IT field. Things became very difficult for him, the bills had accumulated and he fell into debt.

As a close observer, one thing that I found most inspiring is that all this while, my friend continued to hold on to God's promises and never doubted God's ability to resolve his long-standing employment issue. I can recall several occasions during which he encouraged other people who were going through difficult situations, even as he struggled through straitened circumstances.

Several years have passed since then, and now his situation has changed considerably. Miraculously, he got a high-paying job and even pastors a church. He often points to that season in his life as a time when all that he believed was tested.

Five years is a long time, but when we view it from God's perspective of eternity, it is insignificant. One thing is certain, the spiritual impact that season has made on his life will feed into his service of others.

Managing your inadequacies

I have observed that the best leaders are those, who have a very realistic estimation of their abilities and as a result, either work to improve their shortcomings or supplement their deficiencies by hiring staff with the skills they lack. The bible describes Moses as this kind of leader. Though he was well educated and groomed for leadership, when the Lord called him to lead His people out of Egypt, he did not hesitate in highlighting his many weaknesses to God. "But Moses said to the Lord, 'Oh, my Lord, I am not eloquent, either in the past or since you have spoken to your servant, but I am slow of speech and of tongue'." [9] He was acutely aware of his own inadequacies and was aware that even after meeting with God, his weaknesses remained. It goes to show that God chooses to work through us, in spite of our obvious inadequacies. Often times, He does not come to take away our shortcomings, but to show Himself strong despite them. Scriptures are replete with people who were upfront with God about their perceived lack of abilities but whom He used anyway.

God chooses to work through us, in spite of our obvious inadequacies.

God knows our weaknesses and limitations and expects us to acknowledge them, just as Moses did. It is in this humble state that we can accept His grace and find the strength to deal with our inadequacies. God had made provision for the inadequacies of Moses in the person of Aaron, his brother. Aaron became his spokesperson and compensated for Moses' apparent shortcomings.

One way that God ensures that we acknowledge our need for and appreciate other people is through our incompetencies, which force us to admit our limitations and never think ourselves as self-sufficient. God's idea of the Kingdom, is not to have a few wholly self-reliant superstars, but a collective of stars resulting in a beautiful constellation that radiates an even more brilliant light. This is the focus of the next chapter.

CHAPTER SUMMARY

If we're doing anything worthwhile we should expect to have to deal with opposition. We should not let this stop us from continuing with the work.

We may go through challenges even if we are within the will of God. If we are uncertain of the source of the challenge we should pray and seek God, to get confirmation from the word and or through other believers about what action to take.

The challenges we face reveal the true state of our faith in a way that few other things can. If things do not go the way we want, is God still God and, still *our* God at that?

Firstly, in the face of the challenge, we must be persuaded that God is able to deliver us. In scripture Jesus promises to be ever-present, no matter what we are going through

Things are not always going to be easy, often times, one may even feel like quitting. In order to live a significant life we must be well past the point where quitting is a serious option.

Make it Count

The challenges we face could simply be a direct (and expected) opposition by the devil, to the work you're involved in. Prayerfully consider what challenge it is you are facing in the light of the following scripture:

No test or temptation that comes your way is beyond the course of what others have had to face. All you need to remember is that God will never let you down; he'll never let you be pushed past your limit; he'll always be there to help you come through it.- 1 Corinthians 10: 13 (Message)

CHAPTER 8

ONE ANOTHER

None of us can do what all of us can do
- Max Lucado

Bread for myself is a material question.
Bread for my neighbor is a spiritual one.
- Nicholas Berdyaev

For none of us lives for ourselves alone,
and none of us dies for ourselves alone
- Romans 14: 7 (NIV)

U p to this point, I've emphasised the impact you and I can make as individuals as a result of Christ living within us but there's more. In Genesis 2, God introduced the concept of relationships – Adam and

Eve. God observed, "*it is* not good that man should be alone; I will make him a helper comparable to him"[1]. While this was specifically a husband-wife relationship, it points more generally to our human need for relationship. God recognised and sought to fulfil our human need for companionship, sexual pleasure and procreation. This shows us that relationships are God's idea.

Since God created humanity to fellowship with Him, one might be excused for reasoning that Adam's relationship with God should have sufficed. However, God saw Adam's need for a mate, companion and helper. By noting that "it is not good that man should be alone", God was intimating that *no one* should have to be alone.

Having identified Adam's need for companionship, God mentioned only two criteria that such a companion should meet. Firstly, the provision of support or help. And secondly, being complementary but similar, in other words while Adam and his companion, would not be identical they would have many common characteristics. Through their relationship, God made sure that Adam and Eve had everything they needed to succeed. The writer of Ecclesiastes puts it succinctly, "Two people are better off than one, for they can help each other succeed" [2].

Success in life takes more than individual effort. Mother Theresa said, "although one can make a difference, one cannot achieve success all alone". Rarely will you find anyone who stood

Success in life takes more than individual effort

alone and achieved great success, as a result of their sole effort. In his book, *Teamwork 101,* John Maxwell asserts the same thing, "one is too small a number to achieve greatness". He also said, 'you cannot do anything of real value alone' [3]. The reason for these assertions is simple. All you need to do is to take a look at yourself and you will realise that neither you, nor anyone else around you has everything it takes to make an absolute success. Suffice to say, our destinies are connected to one another. When God created man, He did so in such a way that no man would be self-sufficient, hence why He looked at the first man He created and knew that he needed help. We were not made to achieve success all by ourselves.

The bible tells us about a little known king, Jehoram, the son of Jehoshaphat who could have been very successful.

"When Jehoram had ascended the throne of his father and was established, he killed all his brothers with the sword, and also some of the princes of Israel. Jehoram was thirty-two years old when he became king, and he reigned eight years in Jerusalem. And he walked in the way of the kings of Israel, as the house of Ahab had done, for the daughter of Ahab was his wife. And he did what was evil in the sight of the Lord...He was thirty-two years old when he began to reign, and he reigned eight years in Jerusalem. And he departed with no one's regret. They buried him in the city of David, but not in the tombs of the kings". 2 Chronicles 21:4-6, 20 (ESV)

This is a sad story, but offers some very important lessons. When King Jehoram ascended the throne and became established as King of Israel, he decided to kill his brothers and some of the princes of Israel (vs. 13) for fear of being toppled by them. He married the daughter of Ahab, king of Israel, who encouraged him to stray from the Lord. He died after ruling for eight years and the bible notes that no-one mourned his departure. He reigned for eight years but in all that time didn't manage to make any significant positive contribution.

It is likely his insecurities led him down the path of isolation, and as a result he became ineffective. His reign was marked by revolts, enemy invasions and sickness within the royal family (himself included). He had wiped out all the people that could have helped him succeed as king. Right relationships are a key element of success in life, not only to help us achieve success, but also to share our success with.

Types of Relationships

Since relationships are so fundamental to human flourishing, it is important that we understand their dynamics and these, in turn are governed by the nature of the relationships. I believe there are three main types of human relationships, and I explore them below.

Self-serving relationships

If you take a few minutes to study a baby, you will soon realise that the only thing that matters is his or her own needs, and at that age, that is perfectly acceptable. It is however expected that as the child grows, he or she becomes more aware and considerate of the needs of others.

Self-serving relationships are by definition selfish. The main characteristic of selfish relationships is that each party is primarily seeking the satisfaction of his or her own needs. In other words, one or all parties are seeking to receive without paying much attention to the needs of the other(s). Have you ever had people around you who love to talk about their needs, solicit your help in cash or kind, but are never willing to move a finger in support of your interests? Such relationships become draining after a while and often breed resentment. It is because the 'giver' in such a relationship starts to feel used and taken advantage of. Relationships never work well when one or all parties involved act selfishly. I have seen marriages disintegrate, business partnerships collapse and friendships crumble when people insist on pursuing their own selfish interests. Being selfish is the antithesis of the Christian life; they are fundamentally opposed. This is because selfishness puts the focus on self, but giving to or serving others unconditionally (the hallmarks of a Christian life) requires that we take the focus off ourselves and place it on others.

Working together to achieve a common objective falls apart when participants pursue their own selfish interests. When working with other people, the best results are achieved when you do not care who gets the glory, with each person offering their best to ensure the overall success. Winning teams usually imbibe this principle.

Seeing that we are all born with selfish tendencies, growing out of it requires a nurturing environment during the formative years, or a deliberate decision, as an adult, to break free of this natural mindset. The impetus for such a decision often comes from shining the light of God's truth onto the reality of our motives. The bible teaches that we should "do nothing out of selfish ambition or vain conceit. Rather, in humility value others above yourselves..."[4]. Most times, heeding this instruction conflicts with the way we feel, but the more we do so, the easier it becomes to live it out.

Symbiotic

I first heard the word 'symbiotic' during a school biology lesson. It is derived from the word symbiosis, and it describes a relationship in which two organisms depend on one another for sustenance, support, security and satisfaction. In other words, it's a 'quid pro quo relationship' between parties wherein something is given in return for something else. Any interdependent or mutually beneficial relationship between two persons can be described as symbiotic.

A wide range of human relations, personal and informal through to professional and very formal, can be described as symbiotic. These relationships can be on a one-to-basis or between an individual and a group, such as the relationship between a pastor and his or her congregation. Symbiotic relationships aren't static, they are likely to grow and improve as people get to know each other better, or they may gradually deteriorate as people drift apart or needs change.

At a basic level, symbiotic relationships are necessary for human survival, but stronger and purposeful symbiotic relationships offer so much more. They are the essential platform upon which a life of significance is built. Symbiotic relationships foster the sharing and exchange of ideas and values, so great care has to be taken when choosing the people to be in such relationship with. The book of Proverbs states 'He who walks with wise men will be wise, But the companion of fools will be destroyed' [5]. This means that by reason of association, one's life can be enriched or impoverished.

Sacrificial

This is the highest form of relationship. It is a relationship based on giving, not in order to receive but to honour a commitment or a covenant. Few relationships will function at this level because of the personal cost it demands. These types of relationships require the laying down of personal desires or ambitions for the benefit of the other parties. It is this commitment to selflessness that translates a symbiotic relationship into a sacrificial one.

> "Let no one seek his own, but each one the other's well-being" – 1 Corinthians 10: 24

Though Jesus was always committed to His friends and disciples, the relationship they had with Him when He was alive was mainly symbiotic. He served them even as He taught them, fed them, showed them mighty works of miracles and drew them into His surrogate family. They responded by following Him and becoming His friends [6]. They also provided food and other forms of support to Him as well as running errands for Him. While Peter made a verbal commitment of his willingness to sacrifice his life for Jesus, when the first opportunity to stand in solidarity with Christ arose, Peter denounced [7] Him rather than face persecution. However, everything changed for Peter and the other disciples when they understood that Christ sacrificed His life, on the cross, for their sins and those of the whole world. Following Jesus's death, Peter's relationship with the resurrected Christ became one which he was truly willing to die for, and ultimately did. The ministry of the Holy Spirit coupled with the will to see Christ's mission fulfilled through their lives at any cost, resulted in the miraculous and daring events documented in the book of Acts.

For participants in a selfish relationship, the key question is 'how will this relationship serve me?', but in a sacrificial one, it is, 'how can I serve in this relationship?' Christ came and served humanity by sacrificing His life for our sins, and today, over 2000 years later, His legacy lives on. When we genuinely serve others our relationships become sacrificial in nature and we build a legacy that will likely outlive us.

When we genuinely serve others our relationships become sacrificial in nature and we build a legacy that will likely outlive us.

When parties are committed to a sacrificial relationship, service becomes so much more rewarding. The intertwined stories of Naomi and Ruth in the bible demonstrate this perfectly. When Naomi and her family decided to move to the country of Moab in hope of a better life, nothing could have prepared them for the misfortune they would encounter. Naomi lost her husband Elimelech, and then her two sons, Mahlon and Chilion, also died. Following the loss of all she had lived for, she decided to return to Bethlehem, her home town, in pursuit of a better life amongst her people. Whilst in the land of Moab, her sons had married Moabite women, Orpah and Ruth, and so she was left with two daughters-in-law who had also become widows. When Naomi decided to return to Bethlehem, she released her daughters' in-law from their obligation to her. She advised them to stay in Moab with their own people, remarry and start a new life. Orpah decided to heed Naomi's words but Ruth insisted on staying with her. The bible records,

'But Ruth said:

> "Entreat me not to leave you, *Or to* turn back from following after you;
>
> For wherever you go, I will go; And wherever you lodge, I will lodge;
>
> Your people *shall be* my people, And your God, my God. Where you die, I will die, And there will I be buried. The LORD do so to me, and more also,

If *anything but* death parts you and me." Ruth 1:16-17

Ruth's words speak of a commitment to serving Naomi. It was a sacrifice, because Naomi had nothing to offer Ruth at that time. Further given the misfortunes that had befallen Naomi to date, Ruth's decision to follow her might have been considered by many to be asking for trouble!

In Bethlehem, Ruth continued to serve Naomi willingly, and continued to fulfil the duties of a daughter in-law, even though she had been released of her obligations to do so. Her decision to follow and serve Naomi brought Ruth good fortune in the long run. It was as a result of her relationship with Naomi that she met Boaz, a "kinsman redeemer" from Elimelech's (Naomi's late husband) lineage, who decided to marry Ruth. It was this marriage that brought Ruth into the family of Judah, and ultimately the generational line of Jesus.

We do not know what became of Orpah, but we do know that Ruth's decision to make sacrifices because of her love for Naomi brought unexpected rewards and put her name in the family tree of our Lord Jesus.

All parties in a sacrificial relationship win because each one enters into it with an intention to give and serve the other(s).

This is true even though the parties involved may not serve or make sacrifices at the same time.

IMPORTANCE OF SACRIFICIAL RELATIONSHIPS

Cohesive advantage

The motivation for entering into a sacrificial relationship is often love or the achievement of a greater good, rather than what we can get out of it, the truth is we often do get something out of it. In other words, through them we often achieve results that exceed the the sum of the parties' individual efforts. So, when we really commit to working in agreement towards a common purpose with others, we are more than likely to do better than if we were working alone.

The relationships that existed within the early church, as recorded in the bible, is really heart-warming;

> "Now the multitude of those who believed were of one heart and one soul; neither did anyone say that any of the things he possessed was his own, but they had all things in common. And with great power the apostles gave witness to the resurrection of the Lord Jesus. And great grace was upon them all. Nor was there anyone among them who lacked; for all who were possessors of lands or houses sold them, and brought the proceeds of the

things that were sold, and laid *them* at the apostles' feet; and they distributed to each as anyone had need." Acts 4: 32- 35

Here, we learn that the disciples shared their resources and in so doing, were able to meet the needs of those around them. It was a community-instituted welfare program in which everyone benefitted; those who had been blessed with more resources shared their abundance with those that lacked. The result of such cohesive generosity was that many more people came to know and accept Jesus Christ. Talk about living lives that count for eternity! The sacrificial deeds, carried out on a communal-scale, had a significant effect on many lives, far more than if each resource-rich Christian had sought to act alone.

The power of agreement

When ordinary people agree to work together, we get uncommon results. One of the devil's tactics is to cause and foster division, because he knows that where there is division, the power to effect change is short-circuited. In Matthew 12: 25, Jesus Christ said,

When ordinary people agree to work together, we get uncommon results.

"Every kingdom divided against itself is brought to desolation, and every city or house divided against itself will not stand." A divided house is a recipe for destruction, but in a house united around a purpose, you find an unstoppable force able to bring about uncommon results.

The account of the tower of Babel best illustrates the power of agreement. In Genesis 11: 1 – 9, we read:

"Now the whole earth had one language and one speech. And it came to pass, as they journeyed from the east, that they found a plain in the land of Shinar, and they dwelt there. Then they said to one another, "Come, let us make bricks and bake *them* thoroughly." They had brick for stone, and they had asphalt for mortar. And they said, "Come, let us build ourselves a city, and a tower whose top *is* in the heavens; let us make a name for ourselves, lest we be scattered abroad over the face of the whole earth." But the LORD came down to see the city and the tower which the sons of men had built. And the LORD said, "Indeed the people *are* one and they all have one language, and this is what they begin to do; now nothing that they propose to do will be withheld from them. Come, let Us go down and there confuse their language, that they may not

> understand one another's speech." So the LORD scattered them abroad from there over the face of all the earth, and they ceased building the city. Therefore its name is called Babel, because there the LORD confused the language of all the earth; and from there the LORD scattered them abroad over the face of all the earth.

Prior to this event, the whole earth spoke one language. The people of the earth came together with a view to build a commanding city and tower as monuments to self. Their aim was self-aggrandisement. God stopped the work by disrupting the means through which they reached agreement- their language. The fact that He chose to stop their work in this way is interesting. I believe in so doing, God acknowledged the power of commitment to a common purpose; unfortunately in this case, it was deployed for self-serving reasons.

When we put aside our differences and sacrifice our own agendas on the altar of unity, we become an unbeatable force for good. Jesus Christ said in Matthew 18: 19 "Again I say to you that if two of you agree on earth concerning anything that they ask, it will be done for them by My

When we put aside our differences and sacrifice our own agendas on the altar of unity, we become an unbeatable force for good.

Father in heaven". The kind of agreement that Jesus was referring to, is not a casual declaration of interest or agreement to cooperate. He was talking about a much deeper level of commitment. It is this type of commitment amongst the agreeing parties that gets heaven's attention.

The legacy continues

When we serve one another, a culture of service is fostered. In the same way that we plant a seed and anticipate a particular type of harvest, when we serve sacrificially in our relationships, we are sowing seeds that will yield a community of selfless individuals.

Christ served His disciples and charged them to do the same to one another;

> "So when He had washed their feet, taken His garments, and sat down again, He said to them, "Do you know what I have done to you? You call Me Teacher and Lord, and you say well, for *so* I am. If I then, *your* Lord and Teacher, have washed your feet, you also ought to wash one another's feet. For I have given you an example, that you should do as I have done to you. Most assuredly, I say to you, a servant is not greater than his master; nor is he who is sent greater than he who sent him." – John 13: 12 – 16

By washing the feet of His disciples, He showed them that He was willing to serve them in the most humble of ways and urged them to do the same for one another. In those days, it was a task delegated to the lowly servants, to wash the feet of the master of the house, and his guests. The feet would usually be very dirty due to the dust, mud and sweat accumulated during long walks. By washing the feet of His disciples, Jesus was establishing a culture of service amongst them, which was in stark contrast to the culture of the day. That is why thousands of years after His death and resurrection, the message of the gospel is still associated with a life of service.

It is a message that Christians of subsequent generations have sought to embrace, this is why many secular service-oriented organisations today such as the YMCA and Christian Aid all started out with the Christian ethos of serving people.

In 1865, in London's East End, William and Catherine Booth founded the Whitechapel Christian Mission, which later became known as the Salvation Army, to help feed and house the poor. Booth rightly saw the role of church as "loosing [of] the chains of injustice, freeing the captive and oppressed, sharing food and home, clothing the naked, and carrying out family responsibilities." Booth and some

Christian associates chose to practise what they preached by performing self-sacrificing Christian social work. For example, they opened 'Food for the Million' shops (soup kitchens), not caring if they were scoffed at or derided for their work [8]. In his time, many disagreed with his manner and approach, but no one could deny his compassion when faced with the suffering of his fellow man. William and Catherine are long gone, but their work still stands today with many 'Salvationists' serving their communities with the same levels of sacrifice and compassion that their organisation's founders did.

As the saying goes, 'no man is an island'; our interactions and interconnecti vity with others is what makes us truly human.

As the saying goes, 'no man is an island'; our interactions and interconnectivity with others is what makes us truly human. God in His wisdom has ensured that no one is fully self-reliant so that we need to band together in order to live mutually beneficial lives. Only as we serve one another sacrificially do we truly begin to live lives that count.

Sometime ago, my wife told me that she felt we ought to give more, particularly to projects that alleviate the suffering and improve the quality of life of others. To be honest, I was taken aback by this because I felt we were already doing more than enough and our 'charity budget' was fully stretched. As far as I was concerned, given just how self-centred I used to be, I deserved a lot of credit for the remarkable strides I had made towards becoming a blessing to others. However, as a result my wife's generosity and influence I yielded, and I continue to learn to push my limits and to grow in the grace of giving.

Consequently, as we have looked increasingly to meet the needs of others, the Lord has continued to bless us abundantly; even more exciting is the chance to see the difference our giving makes in the lives of others. As we continue to sacrifice for the benefit of others, there is that sense that our life is tending all the more towards a God-honouring and people-impacting life.

CHAPTER SUMMARY

Relationships are God's idea. His intention is that *no one* should have to be alone.

We were not made to achieve success all by ourselves. We were made to work together to achieve God's plans.

Giving to and serving others unconditionally are the hallmarks of the Christian life; our focus should be on others.

When we genuinely serve others our relationships become sacrificial in nature and we build a legacy that will likely outlive us.

When we put aside our differences and sacrifice our own agendas for the good of the team, it becomes an unbeatable force for good.

Make it Count

Consider the impact those in your close circle of relationship have upon you. Identify those that in some way inspire you to live a God-honouring and people-impacting life. Think of ways to invest in these relationships in order to make them stronger.

CHAPTER 9

THE LEGACY OF ONE

The true meaning of life is to plant trees,
under whose shade you do not expect to sit.
- Nelson Henderson

A person first starts to live when
he can live outside himself.
- Albert Einstein

My share in life has been pleasant;
my part has been beautiful
- Psalm 16: 6(NCV)

A s London prepared to host the 2012 Olympics, the 'L' word – legacy- was on many people's lips. Both proponents and opponents were interested in what would happen after the games had come and gone. Many were interested in what would become of the billions of pounds spent on installing mega-sized venues, accommodation and infrastructure, and were unsure whether it would prove to be money well spent on behalf of the future generation.

Usually, when governments are trying to justify the huge expense of hosting the Games, they drum up support amongst citizens before bidding to host it. They talk about the infrastructure and long-term benefits to the city in which it is held. However, in many of the cities that have hosted the Olympic Games, these promised benefits haven't been delivered. In many cases, the venues fell into disrepair due to disuse and neglect, all because the focus during the planning phase was on the successful delivery of the games and not what would happen afterwards.

I was recently on holiday in Greece with my family, our friend and host showed us some of the sites where events had been hosted during the Athens Games in 2004. Regrettably, Athens is yet to enjoy the promised benefits of hosting the Olympic Games. Some have even argued that hosting the Games was a significant contributing factor to the excruciating economic crisis Greece has been suffering since 2009. The Games came and went and in many cases, the decommissioned structures, which are often of no use to surrounding communities, are the only legacy.

I'm sure the organisers and the residents of the host cities hope that the Games will serve as a launchpad for lasting economic, social and physical activity, but this is rarely the case.

It's easy to dismiss the poor legacy of many Olympic Games events as the inevitable folly of government bureaucrats but the truth is that in many cases, we, as citizens are complicit in the process that leads to poor legacy planning. Recently, Sky News anchor, Jeff Randell, presented a documentary called Born Bankrupt. In it, Jeff highlighted how many people are passing a legacy of debt and liability to their descendants; generations yet to be born.

In that documentary, Jeff interviewed Mark Littlewood, the Director General of the Institute of Economic Affairs who said "If you are worried at all, if you have one iota of concern about the environment and climate change, and the sort of planet we are going to leave our children... you should be apoplectic about the level of debt we are leaving them. It is outrageous, it is immoral, but we have lived well beyond our means, and our conclusion is to send our children and our grandchildren and the unconceived the bill for that... He went on to say, "Here's the con. If you are a politician, you want to promise everything you can to the people on the electoral register. The best way to do that is to send the bill to the people who aren't on the electoral register. If you are under the age of 18, or not yet born, you are not on the electoral register. That's what we've done..."[1]

Now, I'm sure some readers will disagree with Littlewood's assessment of the causes of the United Kingdom's national indebtedness. They might cite costly foreign wars or the huge expense of bailing out reckless and irresponsible banks. It is not my intention to make an argument in support of his, or anyone else's, views. Whatever the causes of our current levels of national debt, I think most people will agree that it is the result of decisions we, as a nation, have made over the last few decades. These unsustainable debt levels are the consequences of decision-making based on our present [at the time of making the decision] or near-future and a refusal to seriously grapple with the question of what we'll leave behind when we are gone. The difficulty with leaving a befitting legacy is that it has to do with the future and few of us are good at foretelling or planning for the future. Our preoccupation is often with the present because the rewards are imminent, so we defer anything that has to do with the future, often until it is too late.

What do you want to be remembered for?

A legacy could be a good name or reputation, a family fortune or even one's faith. Few of us give serious thought to the full implications of our daily decisions on the course of our lives, never mind how our life choices will influence what happens after we are gone.

Whether good or bad, every man will leave a legacy behind; but which kind? I have observed that most people only start to think of a legacy as they approach the twilight years of their lives. Such thoughts hardly cross our minds when we are young, as we often reason that we still have much time ahead of us to worry about our legacy.

Few of us give serious thought to how our life choices will influence what happens after we are gone

Jesus lived a relatively short life, but left a legacy that has endured well beyond his lifetime. His life, message and ministry continue to have tremendous impact amongst His followers, and even amongst those who would not describe themselves as Christians. His time on earth was so significant that He became the indicator for locating events in time- BC and AD. His example of leadership and love is modelled the world over. He took twelve uneducated men and transformed most of them into world changers. His life of integrity remains a benchmark for anyone aspiring to leadership. Undeniably, Jesus left his mark on the sands of time and His legacy lives on.

There is an interesting apocryphal story about a man named Father Smith, who lived on an island far removed from the rest of the known world. It happened that unfavourable winds blew a ship off course and it ended up running ashore an island. The sailor and his men had never been to the Island before and out of curiosity decided to explore the island to see if there was any evidence of life on the island. Once they disembarked, they met the inhabitants of the island. Intrigued by the well-being of the people, the sailor asked the chief of the island to explain how they had managed to be so healthy. The chief attributed their health and development to Father Smith. The sailor wanting to find out more asked where Father Smith lived so that he and his team could meet this great man. The chief agreed to take them to where he lived. First, he took them to see the school built by Father Smith, the medical clinic built by Father Smith, then to the dam and irrigation system, developed by Father Smith to power their mills and water the islanders' farms, then past the church built by him to teach the people about God. At this point, the sailor who was so eager to meet with father Smith asked again about seeing Father Smith. The chief led the sailor and his entourage, via a well-worn path to a graveside with a cross, and pointing to it said, 'there lies Father Smith'. Bewildered by this, the captain said, "I asked to see Father Smith and you showed me all the things Father Smith did, and said nothing of his death.

The chief responded that Father Smith had told them of his hope that after his death, he would live on through his legacy and in their hearts. Hence, for the Island dwellers, Father Smith continued with them daily through the many things he did for them.

The things we have accomplished in the service of our own interests die with us, but the things we have done for others will often outlive us. By this, I mean that these things live on as a seed in the hearts of men from generation to generation. Father Smith, though long dead, lived on through his legacy.

What Legacy will you leave behind?
- The Epitaph Principle

I have a very active imagination and sometimes, I imagine the eulogy that might be given at my funeral and what will be written on my tombstone. I know that this is a fairly meaningless activity; I am well aware that it is my daily decisions about how I live my life rather than wishful thinking that will determine what is said about me. The Epitaph principle requires that we live our lives our lives with the end in mind. In other words, each person determines what he or she wants to be remembered for. Very rarely will anyone's tombstone be engraved with unkind words, however accurate and true such words might be. So it's not what's engraved on our headstones that count, but rather the impression we leave on the hearts of those we leave behind.

The story of King Jehoram [2] in the previous chapter also teaches this vital lesson. He lived and ruled for quite a while, yet when he died no one mourned his demise. What a wasted life. I wonder what God's verdict will be concerning such a life. A wise man said; 'the meaning of life is a life of meaning'. King Jehoram lived a meaningless life. This, however wasn't the case with king David. Almost a thousand years following his death, Apostle Paul said of David, 'For David, after *he had served his own generation by the will of God*, fell asleep...' – Acts 13: 36. What a testimony!

Don't sell your birthright.

A while back, I spoke with a gentleman who was facing pressing financial difficulties and as a result spent significant periods of time working away from home. As we spoke, it became evident to me that it was not his straitened financial situation that drove him but a desire to prove himself. Despite the obvious strain his work patterns placed on his family, he ignored their pleas and the advice of friends, to stop. He was, figuratively speaking, willing to sacrifice his family on the altar of ambition. It was quite sad to hear him justify his behaviour on the grounds that it was time for him to pursue his dreams and attempt to make something of his life. It became clear to me that if he continued down this track, his relationship with his family was unlikely to survive the strain. I asked him a question that I regularly ask myself: 'if you were to die today, what would you want to be remembered for, your ambition or a loving family that embraced God because you showed them what it meant to live a God-honouring life?' This is a question worth mulling over.

It seemed to me that this gentleman was, again metaphorically speaking, willing to sell his 'birthright' [in this case, a family that loved him] just as Esau had done. He was willing to forego the real things he could lay claim to and pass on to the next generation for achievements that are fleeting. Jacob and Esau are well-known characters from the bible. As twin brothers born to Isaac (God's promised child to Abraham), each set out to become successful in their chosen vocation. However, as they grew, a distinction which would go on to have a definitive impact on their legacies began to emerge. Esau, the older of the two became preoccupied with immediate gratification and as a result lost out on his birthright as the firstborn when he sold it to his brother for food in a moment of intense hunger.

His birthright was a legacy, his rightful inheritance which, ideally, he should have been able to pass on to his own children at some point. Unfortunately, Esau failed to grasp its value and traded it for something insignificant- a meal. Unlike Esau, we may not so easily be swayed by food, but many people have sacrificed things they should pass on to the next generation, such as their integrity or a good name on the altar of career success. Others have tarnished their legacy by engaging in extramarital affairs, financial misappropriation or other vices for the immediate, but ultimately fleetingly, gratification they offer.

Recent academic research carried out by Oxford and Bristol universities suggests that drinking one or two glasses of wine a week during pregnancy can negatively impact a child's IQ [3].

Some official guidance for pregnant women regarding alcohol consumption suggests that small level of alcohol consumption is acceptable however this research suggests that this simply isn't the case, or at the very least, the risks are difficult to predict. This shows that even things that are within 'legal' limits have the potential to affect future generations. Sometimes it's hard to see how our 'innocent' action could have effects that linger well beyond our time and it is difficult to consider every action in the light of how it may affect our future, but that is exactly what God expects of us to do.

God describes Himself as a transgenerational God. In the bible, He is described as "the God of Abraham, Isaac and Jacob" [4]. In other words, His interest spans generational lines. As Christians, we eagerly await the return of Jesus Christ- to bring an end to all things and to usher in the new heaven and earth. Until His return, we ought to live knowing that our actions and lifestyles pave the way for the generations that may follow after us. It is only in this way that our lives can truly count.

Until His return, we ought to live knowing that our actions and lifestyles pave the way for the generations that may follow after us.

CHAPTER SUMMARY

Are we planning for the future? For the legacy we will leave our descendants?

Few of us give serious thought to the full implications of our daily decisions on the course of our lives, never mind how our life choices will influence what happens after we are gone.

The difficulty with leaving a befitting legacy is that it has to do with the future and few of us are good at foretelling or planning for the future.

Jesus lived a relatively short life, but left a legacy that has endured well beyond his lifetime.

Every person determines what he or she wants to be remembered for. The impression we leave on the hearts of those we leave behind is our legacy.

Make it Count

What will you like to be remembered for? How would you like your epitaph to read?

ENDNOTE

PREFACE

[1] Luke 12: 15

INTRODUCTION

[1] Ecclesiastes 7:2

CHAPTER 1 - GOD STARTS WITH ONE

[1] Genesis 1: 27

[2] Genesis 1: 28

[3] Exodus 3: 10

[4] Joshua 1: 1 - 2

[5] Judges 5: 7

[6] Judges 6

[7] Esther 4 - 8

[8] 1 Samuel 17

[9] Nehemiah 1 - 2

[10] Luke 1: 26 - 38

[11] 1 Corinthians 12: 12 – 14

[12] Judges 13 – 16

[13] Judges 13: 5

[14] Judges 16: 28

[15] Judges 16: 30

CHAPTER 2 - JESUS, THE ULTIMATE ONE.

[1] Genesis 3
[2] 1 Cor. 6:19
[3] Col. 1: 27
[4] Hebrews 1: 3
[5] John 14: 8 – 9
[6] Matthew 9: 36
[7] Luke 2: 49
[8] Matthew 9: 11
[9] Matthew 9: 12 - 13
[10] Luke 7: 34
[11] John 10: 18
[12] Luke 22: 43 – 44
[13] John 14: 6
[14] Joshua 5: 12
[15] Acts 10: 38
[16] Luke 22: 27
[17] John 15: 13
[18] Mason, Mike. The mystery of Marriage: Meditations on the miracle, (Colorado Springs: Multnomah Press, 2006), page 21
[19] Philippians 2: 8
[20] Philippians 2: 9
[21] Psalm 40: 6 - 8
[22] Hebrews 10
[23] John 12: 24
[24] Philippians 2: 9 – 11
[25] Luke 4: 21

CHAPTER 3 - ONE CAN MAKE A DIFFERENCE

[1] Matthew 25: 14 – 30
[2] Matthew 14: 13 – 21
[3] Matthew 25: 28 - 30
[4] Luke 7:3 - 6 (ESV)

CHAPTER 4 - THE IMPACT OF ONE.

[1] Genesis 1: 31
[2] Matthew 18: 1 – 5
[3] Luke 15: 4 – 6
[4] Acts 1: 8
[5] Matthew 25: 35 - 39.
[6] 1 John 3: 17
[7] Exodus 3: 6
[8] Matthew 16: 26
[9] Acts 10

CHAPTER 5 – BECOMING THE ONE

[1] (http://www.wholesomewords.org/missions/bcarey1.html,
   27-08-12, 4.00pm)
[2] Matthew 14: 13 – 21
[3] Matthew 15: 32 - 38

CHAPTER 6 - THE SACRIFICE OF ONE

[1] 2 Corinthians 5: 21
[2] Luke 10: 25 – 37
[3] Luke 10: 27
[4] Luke 12: 13 – 21
[5] Mark 10: 17 – 22
[6] John 12: 24 (NIV)

CHAPTER 7 - THE CHALLENGE OF ONE

[1] 2 Corinthians 7: 5
[2] Quote attributed to C. S. Lewis – "God whispers to us in our pleasures, speaks to us in our conscience, but shouts in our pains: It is His megaphone to rouse a deaf world"
[3] Daniel 3: 29
[4] When You See the Invisible, You Can Do the Impossible – Oral Robert - [Page 57 – 59]
[5] Judges 6: 13
[6] Hebrews 13: 5, Deuteronomy 31: 6, Joshua 1: 5
[7] 1 Samuel 17
[8] 1 Samuel 17: 47
[9] Exodus 4:10 ESV

CHAPTER 8 - ONE ANOTHER

[1] Genesis 2: 18

[2] Ecclesiastes 4: 9 (NLT)

[3] http://johnmaxwellonleadership.com/2011/05/31/
one-is-too-small-a-number/, 08-03-13, 19:09

[4] Philippians 2: 3

[5] Proverbs 13: 20

[6] John 15:15

[7] John 18

[8] http://www.gospeltruth.net/booth/boothbioshort.htm,
08-03-13, 16.29

CHAPTER 9 - THE LEGACY OF ONE

[1] (http://www.if.org.uk/archives/2614/born-bankrupt-sky-
news-tv-hits-the-intergenerational-nail-on-the-head,
17-11-12, 8.00pm)

[2] 2 Chronicles 21:4-6, 20 ESV)

[3] (http://www.ox.ac.uk/media/news_stories/2012/121115.
html, 19-11-12, 8.23am)

[4] Exodus 3: 6

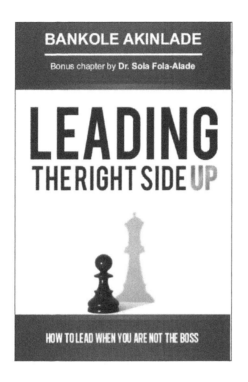

Available to purchase on
Amazon.co.uk
Amazon.com, Borders, Barnes and Noble and other
leading book retailers
www.bankoleakinlade.co.uk

About the Author

Bankole Akinlade serves as the Director of Pastoral Care and Outreach within the leadership team of Trinity Chapel, a vibrant Church based in London. Trinity Chapel seeks to develop leaders who will influence society. Originally trained as a Business Analyst, Bankole has since found his place in Christian ministry. He is most passionate about increasing the impact of Christian service within wider society. He recently completed an MA in Theology, Politics and Faith Based Organisations at Kings College London. His other book, Leading the Right Side Up: How to lead when you are not the Boss has been received with much acclaim in many Christian circles. Bankole enjoys reading and travelling but most of all, he loves spending time with his wife and son.